Praise for *Sex a*

"Smith and Swanson curate accounts of sexual experiences from a diverse group of women, all of whom seem willing to help change the system—or at least the way we talk and think about singledom. Each essay offers a unique perspective . . . themes of both friendship and trauma are threaded throughout the collection, which is mostly respectful to its source material but unafraid of calling out many of its outdated notions." —*Kirkus Reviews*

"*Sex and the Single Woman* is at once a tribute to the groundbreaking work of Helen Gurley Brown and a corrective for her outdated perspectives. With a wonderful assortment of eye-opening, moving stories from a diverse group of writers, the book is a joy to get lost in. Truly a celebration of sexually liberated women—of all backgrounds, ages, and orientations."
—Sari Botton, *New York Times* bestselling editor of *Goodbye to All That* and author of the memoir *And You May Find Yourself . . .*

"*Sex and the Single Woman* is essential reading for anyone who has experienced—or is currently experiencing—all the joys, pains, and complex beauty of their own singlehood era. Rather than painting one's status as a single or childfree woman as something to be pitied or glossed over or devalued, this book takes singlehood seriously and does not contain its exploration to one voice, but rather passes the mic around to paint a much more interesting picture."
—Emma Gray, host of *Love to See It* and author of *A Girl's Guide to Joining the Resistance*

Sex and the Single Woman

Sex and the Single Woman

24 Writers Reimagine
Helen Gurley Brown's Cult Classic

Eliza Smith and Haley Swanson

HARPER ⬤ PERENNIAL

NEW YORK ● LONDON ● TORONTO ● SYDNEY ● NEW DELHI ● AUCKLAND

HARPER ● PERENNIAL

HarperCollins books may be purchased for educational, business, or sales promotional use. For information, please email the Special Markets Department at SPsales@harpercollins.com.

FIRST EDITION

Designed by Jen Overstreet

Author photograph by Cayla Hoskin

Library of Congress Cataloging-in-Publication Data has been applied for.

ISBN 978-0-06-307133-9

22 23 24 25 26 LSC 10 9 8 7 6 5 4 3 2 1

For BJS and LJS

Contents

Sex and the Single Woman

Introduction
Eliza Smith and Haley Swanson

When we met, Eliza was twenty-four and had just moved in with her then-boyfriend, and Haley was twenty-two and quite literally chasing a man across Europe. Things quickly got personal; over our first lunch date, Haley asked if there were wedding bells in Eliza's future, a question Eliza preferred to avoid. Meanwhile, Eliza suspected that Haley's feverish pursuit had far more to do with her own history than any true love connection (spoiler alert: she was right).

Over the eight years since, we've traveled across the country together, celebrated several Friendsgivings, and attended important life events as plus-ones. We've advised each other on health-care plans, impulse buys, haircuts, and questionable apartment features of all kinds (shout-out to Eliza's bathroom with a cramped stall that resembled an industrial freezer more than a shower).

And though our respective relationship statuses have changed, our own bond hasn't faltered. Neither has our interrogation of singlehood. Through it all, we've asked each other—late at night, first thing in the morning, holidays and birthdays especially—what will our lives look like if one or both of us never marry? If neither of us ever has children?

Eliza eventually became so obsessed by these questions that she designed an English course for college first-years on the rhetoric of singlehood. Every semester, she began by explaining why she used the word single*hood* rather than the more colloquial single*dom*. The suffix called to mind other inevitable life stages—childhood, adulthood—implying that being single was not a lesser kingdom to which spinsters were exiled but a phase of life that each of us inhabits for an indeterminate length of time, entering and exiting at intervals, occasionally straddling the line.

Some students were more skeptical of the subject than others. One young woman in particular, who quickly identified herself as a feminist, challenged Eliza from the back row. She felt the course devalued marriage. Eliza thought of herself at her student's age: engaged, grieving a miscarriage, sleeping in her car between classes to avoid the peers who stared openly at her ring.

That's not my intention, Eliza assured her student. *The point is to value the options.*

Eliza had spent the better part of a decade sifting through those options: as a twenty-year-old divorcée starting over in a new city, a twenty-six-year-old leaving behind a perfectly suitable partner for no other reason than she felt she must, a stubbornly independent twenty-nine-year-old so intent on self-sufficiency that she refused to ask close friends for even a brief ride to the airport.

And so, Eliza led her students onward: screening clips from *Bridget Jones's Diary*, *Insecure*, and *Queer Eye*; questioning the romantic motivations in action movies and the differences between being alone and being lonely. She graded more than one paper on the oeuvre of Taylor Swift.

Up next on the syllabus was a twentieth-century throwback.

On May 23, 1962, Helen Gurley Brown's *Sex and the Single Girl*—"the unmarried woman's guide to men, careers, the apartment, diet, fashion, money and men"—innocuously appeared on bookshelves, its plain teal cover and simple serif type in no way hinting at the brazen sex positivity within. Helen's publisher had changed the title from *Sex for the Single Girl* to *Sex and the Single Girl*—anything to smooth over the "vulgarity" of unmarried, sexually active women. (Of course, this was well before Helen, as editor in chief of *Cosmopolitan*, began running now-signature, then-scandalous headlines like "What to Do with (and to) a Sexually Selfish Man.")

That slim volume went on to sell two million copies in its first three weeks. It would be credited—among other texts, most notably Betty Friedan's *The Feminine Mystique*, which was published a year later—with sparking second-wave feminism.

Only a few pages in, Eliza texted Haley: *You have to read this.*

Haley didn't miss a beat in buying her own copy. (We take each other's recommendations with the utmost gravity; no one but Haley could've convinced Eliza to watch CW teen classic *The Vampire Diaries*.) As predicted, Haley flew through the book, tearing up at its closing note: "You, my friend, if you work at it, can be envied the rich, full life possible for the single woman today. It's a good show . . . enjoy it from wherever you are, whether it's two in the balcony or one on the aisle—don't miss *any* of it."

Helen's parting words deeply resonated with Haley. In her

twenties, Haley's mom had been a voice-over agent regularly grabbing cocktails with 1987's brightest upcoming talents. And then the "switch," as she calls it, got flipped: she wanted a baby with the hunger previously reserved for her career.

And so, the family lore of how Haley's mother decided—or rather, felt compelled—to become pregnant framed it as the ultimate choice without choice, a gripping need that a younger Haley feared would one day overtake her, too. She remembers sitting in her adolescent bedroom wondering how much time she had left before her goals of writing and editing in New York City morphed into daydreams of nursery décor and keeping time by her biological clock.

Motherhood, it seemed, was an inevitability.

But now, at thirty, Haley is acutely aware that her "switch" hasn't been flipped. In fact, with each passing day, not only does she expect that innate stirring less and less, but more and more she's questioning why motherhood was framed this way: not as a path sometimes taken after weighing one's options, but as a desire that all women experience and are consumed by, rendering the process of deliberation moot.

However, she did end up getting engaged—though it didn't involve bended knee or compulsory answer. It was a months-long conversation that had more to do with finances and the plan if one of them died (romantic!) than it did with booking a venue for a Saturday wedding in June. The most surprising part of the proposal wasn't the question; rather, it was how there was really no question at all. She and her partner made a decision about their future—together.

And so, the end of her own singlehood era is probably what sent Haley's chin quivering at the close of Helen's book—though she had more than a few gripes with the manifesto's so-called feminist rhetoric that Eliza was also eager to dissect. It couldn't be ignored or glossed over: Helen was a complicated figure, and like all feminist icons, an imperfect one.

Originally pitched as a single girl's guide to having an affair (which in 1962 parlance just meant having sex), Helen's decidedly gleeful advice encompassed pursuing men ("Men like sports; can you afford *not* to?"), getting ahead at work, spending money, cultivating sexiness ("Good health is sexy. Tired girls are tiring!"), styling one's apartment, hosting parties, and cleaving to absurdly elaborate beauty regimens.

With *Sex and the Single Girl*, Helen launched her very particular brand of singlehood, one that told women their unmarried years could be "too rewarding to rush out of" while simultaneously handing them a laundry list of ways to land a husband. Still, like us, Helen seemed to conceive of singlehood as an era, and she wanted women to revel in theirs, including but not limited to enjoying sex. Her radical stance paved the way for narratives like *Murphy Brown*, *Living Single*, and *Sex and the City*.

For the time, Helen's book was damningly provocative. Friedan wasn't alone in describing it as "obscene and horrible," and reading it today can evoke similar responses. Not only does *Sex and the Single Girl* contain messages that feel woefully outdated—such as eliciting expensive gifts from powerful men in the workplace—but Helen's language is also at times racist, homophobic, fatphobic, classist, and ableist. Her recommendations for a life well lived fail to acknowledge her own significant privileges as a cisgender, straight, able-bodied white woman with a wealthy husband and lucrative professional connections.

While many women readers found liberation in those pages—

inclined, perhaps for the first time, to embrace fully realized sex lives, financial independence, and ambitious careers—the end game for Helen, it seemed, was nearly always a traditional, heteronormative pairing.

The book's 2003 reissue featured a new introduction from HGB, eighty-one at the time and living in a new millennium. She acknowledged some of the cultural shifts that had taken place since the sixties, including delayed marriage, queer relationships, and "unconventional" partnerships (meaning those not necessarily punctuated by matrimony or entered into for greater status—in Helen's day, one of few options for women's upward social mobility).

Still, she stood by many of her original assertions, referring to her limited observations as merely "a little quaint."

And so, we wondered: What would a modern *Sex and the Single Girl* look like?

We considered our friends' anecdotes about navigating singlehood, stories from our favorite books and podcasts, essays we'd read on the internet late at night when we should have been sleeping.

The answer was clear: a modern *Sex and the Single Girl* wouldn't be written by only one voice. (And though HGB's use of "girl" wasn't intended pejoratively,[1] we felt ready to move on from that, too.)

If Helen's original message was intended to inspire a specific

---

1   From Helen's 2003 introduction: "(Forgive my continuing to call women girls but I think in many ways we continue to *be* girls all our lives.) At around 25 we often take on adult responsibilities—marry, have children, create homes for other people but I think the basic *girl* is still in there whooshing around—loving fun, being spontaneous, mainlining on enthusiasm, don't you?"

kind of woman to embrace her sexuality and independence—one that, to be sure, resonated with millions of readers at the time— then this anthology is intended to broaden that call, exploring all types of relationships (including solo ones) in the hopes that we can recognize rather than remake ourselves.

In these critical, wry, and expansive essays, twenty-four writers reconsider Helen's advice and how it applies to their own paths of singlehood: the apartments they dwell in, the people they sleep with, the careers they pursue, the bills they pay alone, the fashion they love, the trade-offs they make (again and again and again), the relationships—romantic and otherwise—that sustain them.

Their work also addresses topics that Helen's neglects, including contraception and abortion (an omission demanded by her publisher), queer and trans womanhood, polyamory, interracial dating, bodies of all kinds, consent, singlehood by choice, sex work, IVF and parenting, loneliness, celibacy, and the pop culture that both saves us and fails us. (Not to mention a delightful amount of masturbation.)

Of course, like the original *Sex and the Single Girl*, our version doesn't cover everything we'd like it to. Fortunately, the goal was never to paint a conclusive portrait of single womanhood; it was only to value the options—as Eliza once told her student—by dragging an influential yet narrow text into a modern, more nuanced reality.

Familiarity with the original book isn't required; the first two essays—Brooke Hauser on hearing HGB's voice as she helms a newspaper, and Samantha Allen on Helen's gender policing— address the legacy of both *Sex and the Single Girl* and the woman behind it. From there, we largely leave Helen behind, charting new territory that she couldn't (and wouldn't) conceive of in 1962.

The rich multiplicity of these essays is proof of what we've known all along: we're not the only ones lying awake at night wondering what life might look like if we remain unmarried or without children. In fact, the scales officially tipped in 2009; for the first time, more women are single than married in the United States. And yet representations in our cultural landscape haven't caught up to the lived experience of single womanhood today. We can't yet point to an entire room full of examples and say, *That one, there: that's what I want my life to look like.*

This collection isn't meant to join a chorus of *rah-rah single-hood!* claiming that being unmarried or opting out of parenthood is somehow more hip or even more noble than the alternatives. Some of these writers have never felt more like themselves than they do alone; others are asking for meaningful partnership and the space to develop it alongside their own growth; still more are divided. But all of them are interrogating their deeply rooted conceptions of aloneness.

Partnership, parenthood, and solitude are all paths that take different turns for everyone. None are inevitable, and none are identical. If singlehood is simply a stage that every human must travel through, then the point of these essays is to illuminate what those individual eras of singlehood might look like.

We're ready to discover that roomful of women (preferably a few stadiums full of women, if we're being honest) so we can enjoy the show from wherever we are, as HGB implored. We don't want to miss any of it; we are each other's best witnesses.

And so, we offer up these essays, narratives about living this way, that way, and every way in between, reclaiming joy where it's so often been denied. Our hope is that they capture both who we were and who we want to become.

Her Voice
Brooke Hauser

In the 1960s, Helen taught single women how to
game a system that wasn't built for them. In 2022,
most of us can agree that the solution isn't gaming
the system but changing it to work for all women.

I have a thing for dead women.

It's not as morbid as it sounds. What I mean is that I love
women's history, especially stories about those who've been
underestimated—like Helen Gurley Brown.

Before she died at ninety in August 2012, I was only vaguely
aware of Helen as an eccentric, fishnet-clad relic from the past.
Then I read Margalit Fox's obituary of her in *The New York Times*—
chronicling her rise from small-town girl born in Green Forest,
Arkansas, to Los Angeles copywriter to bestselling author of *Sex and
the Single Girl* and editor of *Cosmopolitan* magazine—and I wanted to
know more.

Helen's hillbilly-to-Hollywood story seemed almost too good
to be true, like it was made for the movies. It kind of was: her husband, David Brown, would become a big-shot movie producer,
turning out hits like *The Sting* and *Jaws*, and I think of HGB as his
biggest production of all. It was David who suggested the idea for

a manual for single girls and, later, a magazine devoted to them. He also advised Helen to publish *Sex and the Single Girl* under her married name, simultaneously giving her an air of respectability and proving that her strategies really worked. But while he set Helen up for success (with the help of her publisher and publicist), she scored on her own merit and message.

In her scholarly biography *Bad Girls Go Everywhere*, Jennifer Scanlon made a compelling case for why Helen deserved a place in feminist history. I wanted to take a more journalistic and cinematic approach to Helen's story, interviewing the people who knew her, loved her, and loathed her. I also wanted to answer the question I always ask when writing about someone in the public eye: Who was she, before she was famous?

The question seemed particularly acute in the case of Helen, who opened *Sex and the Single Girl* with a disclosure about everything she wasn't: "not beautiful, or even pretty," "not bosomy or brilliant"—but also, she confessed, a small-town girl without a college degree who came from a "desperately poor" family. In her words, a mouseburger. "But *I* don't think it's a miracle that I married my husband," she wrote. "I think I deserved him! For seventeen years I worked hard to become the kind of woman who might interest him." (*Seriously?* I thought upon reading her sales pitch, which seemed about as revolutionary as Jell-O salad.)

I decided to focus on Helen's life and career during the sexual revolution and the women's movement of the 1960s and '70s, in part so I could find out: How did Helen become the woman she longed to be? And did she really become that woman for her husband's sake—or for her own? I wondered why I hadn't known more about her when she was alive, especially given that I'd worked in glossy magazines for years in New York City. If she had been such a force, why did she barely register as a footnote in my mind? Why had feminists rejected her? Why had history tossed her aside? These were just some of the questions on my mind when I set out to write what would eventually become my biography of her, *Enter Helen: The Invention of Helen Gurley Brown and the Rise of the Modern Single Woman*.

As it turned out, I had luck on my side: the Helen Gurley Brown papers are housed in the Sophia Smith Collection of Women's History at Smith College, which just so happened to be a few blocks from my then apartment in Northampton, Massachusetts. My husband's job had brought us there, and it didn't take me long to discover the archives on campus. As I read Helen's books and sifted through her handwritten letters, typed manuscripts, clothing receipts, and even her measurements (bust/waist/hips), I was enthralled. And though Helen and I never actually met, I began to feel as if I knew her—or at least the versions of herself she allowed me to know.

When I read *Sex and the Single Girl* for the first time, I was a new mother still wearing a nursing bra and maternity pants. Walking with my infant son on the bike path near my house, one hand on the stroller and the other holding the book, I ate up the opening to her chapter "How to Be Sexy," which read like a prose version of jazz hands with its over-the-top theatrics: *Have you got it? Can you get it? Are you sexy? Let's see*. I could imagine the shock waves Helen set off in 1962 with lines like "What *is* a sexy woman? Very simple. She is a woman who enjoys sex."

Other one-liners had gotten dusty with age. "From nine to five is actually a marvelous time to sink into a man," she wrote in the chapter "Where to Meet Them" ("Them," of course, meaning men). While I cringed at times, I also found places in *Sex and the*

Single Girl where I could nod along or laugh in recognition, particularly at that time of my life: at home with a baby, following an endless cycle of feed, change diaper, sleep, repeat. Women often get the message that ambition is unbecoming, even selfish, and that desiring recognition is unsavory, something that should be concealed. As much as I cherished one-on-one time with my baby, I also yearned to get back to work.

Careerwise, I found an ally in Helen, who was unapologetic about climbing the corporate ladder at a time when women of a certain age were expected to stay home and handle the care and feeding of everyone else. "If you adore your job, men or no men, stay," she wrote. "Getting lost in your work, getting raises, getting recognition—these are some of the all-time thrills."

Those thrills, she added, were "particularly available to single girls who haven't houses, meals on time and the business of dropping off nine pounds of weekly laundry to distract them."

In other words, maybe those thrills weren't particularly available to me.

To write about Helen's life, I wanted to channel her writing voice, which ranged from sex kitten to saleswoman to sophisticated older friend, with a dash of Louella Parsons thrown in ("nothingburger," anyone?). I grew to recognize her style and syntax in her handwritten letters ("Dear Pussycat") and *Cosmo* columns (she *adored* italics, CAPS, and exclamation points!). But it was *Sex and the Single Girl* where she first mastered the art of being both self-possessed and self-effacing, all while slipping controversial ideas into coy packages. (It's hard to feel threatened by a woman who uses "pippy-poo" as an adjective.) While I quibbled with her use of the word *girls* (especially when men were just . . . men), I realized that the girlish phrases with which she lured in her audience were all in the service of a larger message: that single women had sex, liked it, and shouldn't be ashamed of it. In the early 1960s, that took guts.

I also studied Helen's speaking voice in taped interviews and her 1963 advice album, *Lessons in Love*, its two sides tellingly titled "How to Love a Girl" and "How to Love a Man." "I think life is *luscious* when you're a girl, and the most luscious part of all is loving a man," she says breathily on one track. By the time I started interviewing people who knew Helen, I could hear her in my head, the voice she'd molded and modulated over time to be "sexy and oomphy." She gave her single girls tips on how to do the same: "About your telephone voice . . . or any-other-time voice, it's a tough assignment to change its timbre, but movie stars have sometimes lowered theirs a whole register," she wrote in *Sex and the Single Girl*, advising readers to study celebrity voices in order to revise a nasal tone or squeaky pitch. "Most of them were willed into being by practice, practice, practice."

Helen had one of those voices that gets stuck in your head like a song—or a jingle.

In 1965, Joan Didion wrote in *The Saturday Evening Post* that it was a voice made for the airwaves, a "calculating provocative voice" that alternately shocked and seduced the public as she described offices as the sexiest places in the world but warned readers that bosses make lousy lovers. Gloria Steinem lambasted Helen's style in the *New York Herald Tribune* as "an ingenious combination of woman's-magazine-bad and advertising-agency-bad."

And Nora Ephron captured it five years later in *Esquire*, quoting Helen on the importance of self-help and making oneself "more cupcakable all the time so that you're a better cupcake to be gobbled up." That's how Helen spoke when she got carried away, Ephron noted: "exhortation, but in the style of girlish advertising copy."

Even after publishing *Enter Helen* in 2016, I continued to hear her voice. Sometimes, I listened. Other times, I shut it out.

Her voice was there several years ago when I found myself jobless after a women's magazine I'd been freelancing for switched editors and my contract abruptly ended. "A career is the greatest preparation for marriage," Helen had written, noting that a nine-to-five could make working "girls" better organized *and* better at pleasing men. (I know—insert eye-roll emoji.) Soon, with two young children at home, I found the opposite to be true: marriage and motherhood had further prepared me for a journalism career that required the ability to multitask and make split-second decisions. When my neighbor clipped out a call for an arts and culture editor at our community newspaper for me, I jumped on it and landed the job. Once I had arranged childcare for my baby daughter, I showed up for my first day of work, hair blown out straight and maternity pants traded in for a pair with an actual waistband.

At first, I was scared I would hate my new nine-to-five; I'd gotten used to working at my own pace while freelancing. But I found that I liked the job, despite or even because of its quirks. When my trash bin started overflowing, I asked when the janitor would come by and was surprised to learn that along with assigning, editing, writing, and proofing stories, we were also responsible for dumping our own garbage into a communal bin. At such moments, I heard Helen's voice in my ear: "Don't demand instant glamour . . . Keep your shirt on! Give yourself time to get useful before you get difficult."

There would be no glamour, instant or otherwise. Nonetheless, I loved making a newspaper with my colleagues and my community. And I was mesmerized by the power of the 220-ton printing press, which astounded many who saw it. How awesome that words you'd written—in some cases only minutes before—could be transferred to print and be flying through the machine at lightning speed. I started going back to the pressroom regularly to collect the pages I had just edited, as they say, hot off the press.

Before I knew it, a year had passed, and I was applying for the vacant position of top editor.

It felt like a big step, and it was. I had plenty of experience reporting, writing, and editing for various publications, but I had never managed an entire newspaper—or an entire staff, for that matter. Some of those staffers had deep roots at the paper and in the community, whereas I was a more recent transplant. Part of what I had to offer, though, was a fresh perspective and new ideas for connecting with potential readers, in addition to lifelong subscribers.

The interview process was involved. I spent hours in extensive discussions. I critiqued past editions and brainstormed ideas for what the paper could and should be. The closer I got to landing the job, the more nervous I became about all that it would entail.

Needing some moral support, I consulted those closest to me: my husband, my parents, my neighbor who'd clipped that job listing . . . and Helen Gurley Brown. I thought back to how she'd taken over *Cosmopolitan* having "never so much as worked in the mailroom of a magazine, let alone edited one," as *Life* magazine put it in 1965. If she could lead a national magazine with little to no editorial experience under her belt, why couldn't I lead a local newspaper with nearly twenty years of editorial experience under mine?

Founded in 1886, *Cosmopolitan* had gone through several incarnations over the years, from family journal to literary magazine to general-interest publication. By the mid-1960s, it was in the midst of an identity crisis when Helen and David approached Hearst to pitch a magazine for single women called *Femme*—essentially *Sex and the Single Girl* repackaged as a monthly—with Helen as its editor in chief. Instead of launching a new title, Hearst decided to give *Cosmopolitan* a makeover, using the Browns' *Femme* proposal as a blueprint. All Helen had to do now was learn how to put out a magazine.

She leaned heavily on David, who had been a managing editor at *Cosmopolitan* before he was appointed, in 1951, to head the story department of 20th Century Fox in California. Still, despite the significant and undeniable leg up, it was Helen's steeliness (underneath the kittenish exterior), her sheer will, and her connection with readers that catapulted *Cosmo* into phenomenal financial and popular success. Within a few months at the helm, Helen had turned the magazine around, reaching the million-copy mark in circulation and bringing forth "a flood of new advertising," *Life* wrote, calling the transformation "one of the fastest and most remarkable successes in the history of publishing."

It was a PR victory for Helen, who faced her share of critics when she first started. In the eyes of some staffers, she was an impostor, a pseudocelebrity who'd gotten famous off a sex book and had no business running a national magazine. But they underestimated both Helen's drive and the power of her brand. Every editorial decision she made was in service of her *Cosmo* Girl—a single, small-town young woman who dreamed of making it big someday—a reader she knew intimately because, as she put it, "I *was* that girl." It was a blueprint that worked.

"Members of the staff quickly discovered that Helen's terribly polite, terribly innocent, terribly quiet exterior was a convenient and effective cover for a terribly determined and terribly ambitious interior," read the article in *Life*, floating a new nickname for her in its headline—"The Soaring Success of the Iron Butterfly."

In the end, I got the job, which made me the first woman in the role on a permanent basis since the paper's founding in 1786. I heard Helen's voice, one editor in chief congratulating another, and I went on hearing it.

During the negotiation process, I vaguely recalled her advice about raises: "It is up to a company to pay you as little as it can and still get you to stay (any company that makes a profit, that is)." I made sure my salary was commensurate with my years of experience.

I heard her again each time I saved money on a line in the budget—and each time I spent too much on a snack from the vending machine or a takeout lunch. Helen proselytized about the virtues of bringing a brown-bag lunch from home—so much better for your wallet *and* your waist—even suggesting several plans for these "American Beauty Lunches" in *Sex and the Office*. While my stomach turns to read her recipe for Mother Brown's Rich Dessert Tuna Salad, I started keeping a paring knife and plastic spoons in my desk drawer, per her recommendation; they came in handy whenever I prepared a healthy lunch of sliced apple, granola, and yogurt.

I heard Helen whenever I wrote an editor's note giving readers a glimpse into the newsroom or my own thought process, as she did so well with her longtime *Cosmo* column, "Step into My Parlor," and I thought of her every time I chose a simple word over a fussy one. ("Why say 'myriad' if you mean 'many'?" I chided reporters. "Don't say 'establishment'; just say 'bar.'") She liked to make potentially complicated subjects "baby simple" in order to reach as many readers as possible. While I would never use that phrase (or "piffle-poofle," for that matter), I felt we had a responsibility as a community newspaper to be as clear as possible for depth of understanding and breadth of reach. By all means, capture the complexity of an issue or debate, but when it comes to giving readers a primer—whether it's explaining a new sex position or the details of a proposed property tax override—you'd better get to the point.

But that's where our similarities as editors end. As much as I appreciate Helen's can-do spirit, she made plenty of regrettable editorial moves. At *Cosmo*, she was known to publish fake case histories and letters to the editor, not to mention phony diets. A former staffer I interviewed recalled concocting one involving grapefruit and hard-boiled eggs.

Helen was also wrong about graver matters. In the 1980s, she ran a story in *Cosmo* downplaying the risk of straight women contracting HIV; the article was written by a psychiatrist with no proven medical expertise regarding the virus, and it led to a large protest outside the Hearst building. She loved rich and powerful men, and she often gave them a free pass. In the 1990s, she made light of sexual harassment amid charges against Supreme Court nominee Clarence Thomas and Senator Bob Packwood. Asked whether any women staffers at *Cosmo* had been sexually harassed at work, she tried to be cute but came off as crass and archaic, saying, "I certainly hope so."

In short, if Helen was alive and in power today, she'd probably be canceled.

Ten years have passed since Helen and I first "met," and she still fascinates me. Her artifice—or self-invention—is a big part of the attraction. Something about it seemed to get under people's skin. In 1982, the year Helen published *Having It All*, Gloria Steinem interviewed Helen for a cable TV special. "I think you have secrets and a seriousness and a worth that *Cosmo* as a magazine doesn't adequately reflect," Gloria told her. "That your public image doesn't adequately reflect."

She was right, of course, but it was an image that Helen herself—with help from her producer husband—had created, then edited, again and again. Who *was* the real Helen? It's impossible to know. She revised everything from her voice (practice, practice, practice) to her face (with plastic surgery and silicone injections) to her personal story (she wasn't from a "hillbilly" family, after all; her mother had been a schoolteacher, her father a budding politician before he died in an accident that changed the course of her life). Her papers collected at the Smith College archives should be considered in this light, elucidating between rough draft and revision—she was, after all, an editor. A *Cosmo* colleague who likened Helen's many faces to a Picasso painting cautioned me: "When it seems to you as though she's being a storyteller, she is."

While Helen did her share of self-revision, the passage of time has also played a part in how she's remembered—or not.

After my book came out in 2016, there was some renewed debate about whether Helen was a feminist. It's a question she answered herself over the years—and she revised her opinion on that, too. In her June 1970 editor's letter in *Cosmo*, Helen explained her position on the women's lib movement. "Like many other women, I've come to respect it late in the day," she wrote, noting that, at first, she thought it was "just an attack by a few hostile nutburgers who were giving *all* women a bad name." Eventually, she came so far around as to call herself a "devout feminist." Still, I think of her mostly as an opportunist.

I no longer work at the community newspaper, and I'd be lying if I said that I think of Helen much in my new routine, freelance writing and editing from home until it's time to pick up the kids from school. (Remember, this is a woman who once advised her single girls to "borrow children" for weekend entertainment or to perform the occasional chore.)

Still, I have been thinking a lot about the role of an editor in general. The best ones have a vision, not just for the publication they're editing but for how they want the world to be. Helen had a vision, but it was a tunnel vision. She wanted single women to lead rich, fulfilling lives . . . so they would be better positioned to attract and keep a man.

When I read *Sex and the Single Girl* today, in my forties, I see it not as some racy manual but as a survival guide on how to be successful in a world that caters to men. In the 1960s, Helen taught single women how to game a system that wasn't built for them. In 2022, most of us can agree that the solution isn't gaming the system but changing it to work for all women—not just those who are white, single, straight, and cisgender. As Suzanne Levin, a former editor of *Ms.* magazine, put it in *The New York Times* in 1974,

"*Cosmopolitan* is talking to women one by one. We're talking about making all women's lives work."

Which includes mothers—whether we work for pay or not. My goals and curiosity about the world around me didn't disappear with the birth of my children; my days didn't narrow into simply "dropping off nine pounds of weekly laundry," as Helen so pointedly wrote. (And anyway, I do my own laundry.)

In many ways, we still live in a "man's world," where men in high offices can make life-altering decisions about our bodies, workplace equality is hardly a given, and we shoulder the bulk of unpaid labor at home. But it's not 1962, and in the wake of #MeToo, Black Lives Matter, and the COVID-19 pandemic, women are speaking up and out, demanding change—a global chorus of voices that's wonderfully cacophonous and loud.

Perhaps that's why lately, when I hear Helen's voice, it sounds small—and very far away.

When a Man Isn't a Man
Samantha Allen

In reality, singlehood is all of us failing
each other, over and over again, in ways that
sometimes teach us things about ourselves but
can also leave us feeling broken and alone.

"How do you tell when a man isn't a man?"

Helen Gurley Brown meant the question playfully, I'm sure, when she used it to open the "homosexuals" section in *Sex and the Single Girl*. But despite the performative flippancy—or perhaps even more so because of it—it still echoes uncomfortably today. Brown's bon mot implies that gay men aren't really men, which is still the prevailing view in many quarters. Sometimes that sentiment is expressed in overtly homophobic ways—slurs shouted across the street—but it's also present in the straight woman who considers her gay best friend to be "just another one of the girls." (Brown herself helped usher in the age of the GBF by recommending gay men as "wonderful friends—loyal, sympathetic, and entertaining.")

But Brown's question also suggests, more tacitly and I think more insidiously, that it's a woman's job to suss out men who don't conform to gendered expectations. "How do you tell when a man isn't a man?" implies that *you*, the reader of *Sex and the Single Girl*, are the one who should be doing the discerning and defining. Here's your badge, you're deputized, now go play gender detective. "Use your instinct," Brown recommends. Examine his living situation, his relationship with his mother, and his stance toward other men. If things don't add up, there's only one possible conclusion in Brown's wry parlance: "He's a girl."

But sometimes "He's a girl" turns out to be a more literal explanation. Before I transitioned from male to female, the women I dated certainly asked Brown's question about me. Not out loud, at least not right away. First their probing took the form of furrowed brows and searching eyes. What, exactly, was I? A little bit gay? A cross-dresser? Something worse? Under their scrutiny, I felt like I was coming undone while being expected to prove my wholeness—as though someone were pressing down hard on my navel and asking me to do jumping jacks at the same time.

It was withering to be on the other side of that skepticism while still in the closet. When the girls I liked in middle school told me they wished I could come to their sleepovers because I was "more like a girlfriend," part of me wanted that to be true—and another part of me wanted to deny it. The women I dated in college—most of whom knew I "cross-dressed," as I rationalized it at the time—could sense that I was happier presenting female than I ever was in our humdrum and ostensibly heterosexual day-to-day. As that realization dawned on them, their faces fell. I couldn't be what they needed me to be.

I was a man who wasn't a man.

I was only able to admit that to myself at age twenty-four, mostly because I didn't fully understand the word *transgender* until then. But I never really felt like a man, either—and I said as much to the women who got close to me. Based on their reactions, they seemed to think I was spouting some bullshit college-dorm philosophy, as though I were taking a hit off a joint and saying, "I don't believe in labels." Perhaps they mentally added some words to my admission and told themselves that I wasn't a man in *a traditional sense*—that I didn't relate to some hegemonic archetype of masculinity—and that this was a good thing.

I could've been more forthcoming, too. Expressed myself at greater length. But reliably, around the six-to-eight-month mark, my girlfriends all realized I was trying—fumbling, really—to express some deep sense of dissonance between my soul and my flesh. In their minds, "I don't feel like a man" went from signaling "My boyfriend isn't an asshole" to "My boyfriend might be gay." I felt not just the discomfort at coming closer to being seen, but the guilt of having failed them.

When I broke up with the woman I dated in graduate school because I realized I couldn't deliver the life she wanted, she croaked out the question, "Who will be with me now?" as though I'd locked her outside during a zombie apocalypse. I cried with her, unable to answer, not because I didn't think she'd ever find anyone else, but because I couldn't bear the weight placed on the moment. I hated that she felt like her options for intimacy were narrowing because I was leaving. I didn't want to be the cause of anyone's loneliness.

But I was also in an impossible predicament. If I wanted to be with women, which I did, I thought I had to be a man. So I wanted to be a man—wanted to prove that *I could be* a man—because I didn't know it was an option for someone born with my parts to be a woman, let alone a queer woman. Women also wanted me to be a man, because word was datable men were scarce. Between this sentiment (or as Brown so cleverly put it, "Husbands and daddy-replacements are admittedly hard to find") and the adage that "All the good ones are gay," I learned that there weren't enough quality straight men in the world to go around. And although I'm not sure I would consider myself "good," I wasn't awful—I could be selfish, sure, but I was also romantic, witty, and smart—and apparently that made it more imperative for me to be a man.

I owed it to women to at least try to be one of the good ones, I thought. That internal calculus was mind-numbingly complicated, requiring me to balance who I wanted to be with the people I wanted to date. I was caught in a veritable cat's cradle of gendered expectations, some of them my own, others externally imposed.

As with many emotional dilemmas that seem inescapable in the moment, it was possible to simply step outside of mine once I found my footing. Transitioning from one gender to another can feel almost like a baptism, a cleansing of a past life that in my case was filled with no fewer than six relationships doomed from the start due to a mismatch of sexual orientations and gender identities. And so I was able to leave behind the agony and angst of that half decade of dating. Those years felt heavy, leaden—and then they were washed away. There was no point being upset about them any longer.

My present is simple: I'm a woman married to a woman who's attracted to women—a beautiful, parsimonious alignment of body and desire. But I do count myself among those affected by a *Cosmo* era that lived on in our cultural imagination much longer than it should have. It's not the 1960s anymore, neither socially nor economically, and it's taken us a long time to admit it. A sexual revolution was a fun party to have while the country was still flush with postwar cash, when HIV was unknown, and before capitalism sucked all the joy out of life, leaving us to slurp desperately at the straw of entertainment for some simulacrum of abiding pleasure.

Today, as I watch overworked friends with empty refrigerators swipe away at dating apps, restless and afraid about the future, it's hard to believe we even live in the same America that Brown once saw as a sexual playground. In 2022, everyone has a pocketful of "availables"—no need to read a chapter in a book about "where to meet them," no point driving around in "heavy traffic" trawling for "possibilities"—but few people of any gender seem all that happy about the convenience. A majority of women and a plurality of men, the Pew Research Center recently found, believe dating is harder today than it was ten years ago, and declining percentages of young people report having casual sex.

I can add to this my own anecdotal finding that many over-educated eligible straight women preferred being in a relationship with a closeted transsexual writer to the supposed delights of modern singledom. For many of us, unattached life isn't exactly the carnival ride that *Sex and the Single Girl* promised it could be.

Not that Brown is anything close to being the architect of our current nightmare. HGB didn't turn income inequality into a gaping maw between the rich and the poor, nor did she engineer the looming sense of alienation that grew larger as smartphones got smaller. Some of the central ideas that she championed in her breakout book—and over the course of her long magazine career—were good at their core: women should take pleasure in and more ownership over sex.

But in the wake of the sexual revolution, debates between the third-wave feminism that Brown foretold and the antifeminism typified by Phyllis Schlafly almost always seem to get caught in a frustrating dialectic, the former ideology promising that a full decade of adult singledom is rewarding and right, the latter maintaining that it is unsatisfying and wrong, neither of them able to acknowledge the banal truth that forces beyond the cultural—stagnating wages, rising health-care costs, lengthening work weeks—are turning both early marriage and casual sex into joyless pursuits.

What Brown is partially culpable for, though, is perpetuating the same culture of dehumanization that made her book so necessary in the first place. *Sex and the Single Girl* arrived at a moment when men had long been treating women like snacks to categorize and consume—but instead of encouraging women to exercise sexual agency differently, it talked to its presumed reader like a big-game hunter about to go on safari. It spoke about relationships in financial terms, referring to marriage as "insurance," claiming that the men one encountered along the way to a husband were "cheaper emotionally"—seemingly all in good fun. However, that framing isn't without its costs, so to speak. The book committed the classic mistake that *Lean In* did fifty years later, urging women to play the game harder instead of flipping over the table.

As a transgender woman who tried to make sense of herself against the confusing backdrop of a world in which men and women were chasing each other, I'm just one of many of that attitude's discontents. "You do need a man of course every step of the way," Brown famously urged, and in so doing helped usher in a world where we're no longer rushing to marry before we're old enough to rent cars, but in which we're still trying to derive too much fulfillment from the people we fuck.

I might have failed the women who couldn't tell right away that

I wasn't a man, but they were failed, too—we all were—by a discourse that told us sex and relationships were the essential project of early life, that we couldn't imagine happiness that didn't center around them. "Of course" you need them, "every step of the way," Brown says—and that "of course" does a lot of heavy lifting. It's the rhetorical equivalent of saying "just because." Sometimes it feels like we're in a nightclub being pumped full of thumping, buoyant house music when we'd all rather go to sleep, but no one wants to admit they're not having fun anymore because isn't this where we're supposed to be?

Our media, from *Sex and the Single Girl* to *Sex and the City* all the way down to *Girls* and *The Bold Type*, still depict unattached urban life as a romp-filled bildungsroman, each encounter a step toward self-actualization. In reality, singlehood is all of us failing each other, over and over again, in ways that sometimes teach us things about ourselves but can also leave us feeling broken and alone. Alone because things are missing from our lives that no person can provide and that no person should bear the burden of providing. Because even marrying my ideal person hasn't made me whole.

"It's not always easy to tell a homosexual even if you have a suspicious nature," Brown advised, and I came of age under that suspicion, like a fern growing in shade, because women were trying to find out if I really was the man I tried to convince myself I could be. Like many in my generation, we weren't joyful participants in some carnal buffet; we were leaning on each other because we didn't know what else to do. We watched the fading embers of the sexual revolution blink out altogether while our world grew less certain, less secure, and less tangible—and then we stared at the ashes instead of starting fires.

I think back to those indefinable relationships and encounters now—points of contact between women looking for a man and a transgender woman trying to be one—and I look for the "queer art" in their inevitable failure, as the queer theorist Jack Halberstam once proposed. I lost, but in losing, I've "imagined other goals for life, for love, for art, and for being." I got to gather kindling for other kinds of fires—for writing, for travel, for solitary pleasures.

Hidden in Brown's "of course" was a heteronormative injunction: Just do it. Literally. But the moment we accept the unsustainability of that imperative—the moment we acknowledge that singlehood is failure but so, too, is sex, and that to have a gender is to fail at gender—we can begin to see ourselves and others differently, not as options at a cafeteria that will never fill us up, not as what Brown terms "availables," but as people trying our best in a much less optimistic decade than the one into which *Sex and the Single Girl* was born.

"How do you tell when a man isn't a man?" is what I wish I'd asked myself during those early years, back when we all could've been mulling over questions instead of looking for answers in the arms of others.

The "Straight" Girl
Shayla Lawson

For years I'd been called toward the divinely
feminine, but now, I was finally seeking it.

In seventh grade, I pulled up a *Seventeen* magazine using my
middle school library's card catalog. In the issue, littered with
homoerotic Tampax pillow fights and an ad for dELiA*s, an advice
columnist answered a reader's question indexed under the topic
"GAY."

Am I gay? the pull-quote read, dead center of the page. I remember slinking into the orange-pilled cushions of the library
couch, chest swarming hot with butterflies. I pulled the magazine
tight around my face, fingers on the fold like a hair trigger, so I
could quickly switch to an article on Jonathan Taylor Thomas if
any kids walked by. (In the issue, an adult reporter asked him how
he felt about being a teenage heartthrob and what special girl he
was into—which JTT answered by talking about recipes he was
working up at home with his new favorite spice, lemon pepper.)

But the adolescent sexual inquiry I was focused on read something like this: *Hi, I'm thirteen. I like boys but I get really turned on
watching the women in sex scenes from action movies. Does that make
me gay?*

I was twelve and only allowed to see PG-13 movies with my mom. Which was cool because she liked big-budget action flicks where emotionally unavailable men blew things up, but awkward because these men would usually encounter really smoking, sweaty, independent women. They'd lustily throw each other up against hotel walls while I covered my eyes so I wouldn't catch any of this "adult content"—when I was actually shielding my face because I was worried that even in the dark she might catch the heat in my warm, brown blush.

I tried continually to pretend alongside other girls that I had crushes on adult male celebrities like Denzel Washington, Will Smith, Brad Pitt, and Joaquin Phoenix, but really, I liked boys my own age: the middle brother in *The Three Ninjas*, a tall kid in the back of my Spanish class, a boy in my Bible study group . . .

And most sexy older women.

I read on.

The *Seventeen* article was gracious and—I thought at the time—a bit progressive, in that it very patiently described to the curious reader that although it was okay for her to be gay, simply getting turned on by hot women in action films probably meant nothing, because all girls and women are *so accustomed to responding to the male gaze that they can receive the same erotic response from seeing attractive women out of "aesthetic appreciation" of the female form.*

So, that was that. I was straight for the next twenty years.

I had my first kiss at eighteen with a boy who wore flowers in his long hair; for the next few years, he would be my on-again, off-again boyfriend. I was a virgin (which explains a lot of the on-again, off-again) and would remain so until I married at twenty-eight. So many of my relationships with guys and friendships with girls maintained the same level of codependent intimacy: holding hands, sharing stories, painting nails, and cuddling while listening to records. Only with boys would I plunge into the occasional make-out sessions or heavy-petting experiments.

But in the nineties, there was a lot of wiggle room for homoerotic behavior between women. On television, kissing, wrestling, and an absurd amount of intense eye contact with your BFF was just par for the course, as depicted in *Seinfeld*, *Murphy Brown*, *My So-Called Life*, and *Buffy the Vampire Slayer*. I would sneak snippets of these shows, since my overprotective parents still expected me to watch only the Disney Channel, PBS, or daytime BET. From what I could gather through glimpses, popular '90s high school catchphrases, and the occasional commercial, shows portrayed feminine intimacies as seriously queer.

Jordan Catalano, the depressed love interest in *My So-Called Life*, with his lipstick, eyeliner, and deeply pouty thumb bite when thinking about something important? Picturing him *still* gives me intense butch-baby androgyny, genderqueer vibes. The scenes where Catalano-obsessed Angela Chase and her bestie Rayanne Graff would try on makeup while feeling each other up, and Rayanne would talk about how firm Angela's mom's boobs were? Let's not play; all three of those kids were definitely thinking about knocking boots together. Then there was *Buffy the Vampire Slayer*. The show eventually featured a bona fide bisexual character in former teen werewolf-lover Willow, but before that, Buffy and fellow slayer Faith would tussle to what I can only imagine as the titillation of all in the female-appreciation persuasion.

Only one problem: these examples were white women. For them, experimenting with romantic fluidity during sexual development was normal, particularly for those who were thin or involved in cheerleading at one point or another. However, Black girls who flirted with their sexual desires, seeing a wide skirt of possibility, didn't appear for me outside Suge Avery in *The Color Purple*. And even when I saw Suge, I totally missed the point.

They're not gay, they're just good friends, I remember telling a classmate in my late teens, trying to protect the two characters played by Whoopi Goldberg and Margaret Avery in the '80s film adaptation I watched on VHS.

I'm not saying this was everyone's world, but it was mine.

The first time a woman hit on me, I was twenty-one and studying abroad in Venice, Italy. The year was 2002; "I Kissed a Girl" by Katy Perry was still six years away from radio play.

I was in a bar having drinks with a group of southern, conservative male classmates when a messy-haired sculptor in heavy eyeliner and lipstick came up to me. I had my own hair done up in a Grace Jones–style pompadour. We were both wearing all black, like sexy action dolls. I leaned into the excitement of the moment, invigorated by the possibility of what being hit on by my very own girl would feel like.

And it felt . . . banal.

She talked—as I'd grown accustomed to older men doing—about how much money she made and the property she owned. I played dumb because the conversation felt so misogynistic and ordinary. She walked away, and twenty minutes later, proceeded to make out with a brunette at the opposite end of the bar. All the American college boys I was with cheered and applauded as if they were joining in to sing "Happy Birthday" to a stranger at a restaurant.

Just think, that could have been you, one of them said before turning back to his beer. His comment was meant to be lewd but hearing it felt more like relief to me. As a Black girl, I worked very hard to be seen as ordinary. To keep even my heterosexuality from being on display to the world. Being seen as too nice, too good, or too sexless to make out with a woman at a bar afforded me an invisibility that felt like liberation from the prospect of being judged by men, or worse. His remark was a veiled warning about something he, as a young, collected southern gentleman, could neither condone nor protect—my feminine sexual agency. As long as I was "straight," this type of man might offer me protection from worse men. So, when it came to being straight, I passed.

And I went on passing for the rest of college and into adulthood. Much like the narrator of Katy Perry's future hit, the only girls I knew who weren't openly gay but talked about being attracted to other girls—or at least hooking up with them—did so to satisfy men's lust. For them, being attracted to women was a way to wink at danger, to live on the edge, to be wild—all things my dark skin coded me as having to work against in order to be loved by anyone, including my parents.

So, I kept a quiet and careful distance from being in love with women. Still a virgin through my early and midtwenties, the attraction I felt toward others was soft, intimate, and deeply romantic. In accordance with the article from my teen years, I assumed my deep "appreciation" for women was nothing more than a highly refined aesthetic for beauty.

And truthfully, I still believe that's what great sex is—a highly refined aesthetic. But I wouldn't even begin to explore that need in myself until my marriage ended in 2015 and I entered the world as a newly divorced former housewife. Once I didn't have to perform as anyone's perfect "good girl" or a model Stepford wife, I gleefully became involved with a married couple I met through mutual friends.

I knew the threesomes were manifestations of more than just curiosity, but an intense love I had for multiple genders. In fact, copulative sex was rarely a part of it. Instead, there were candles, bubble baths, massages. There was a lot of cuddling on absurdly oversized furniture, and good food and wine. There was dancing as a threesome in the basement of a restaurant that looked like an Elks Lodge and sometimes played oldies music, during which—I'll never forget—a woman we didn't know tapped one of us on the arm and said, *Excuse me. They're not even playing a slow song.*

Despite everything I'd been taught, my foray into the wider world of sex with women had nothing to do with being degraded. It was, in the cinematic sense, as soft a landing as my honeymoon night, my new husband untethering each hook and eye on my corseted wedding gown. Only this time, I didn't do it for any man.

In fact, the male principal usually played as much of a supporting role in these new sex equations as Buffy's dude pal Xander. What I was learning was that we all share this wide world of bodies and pleasure that can be kind, and plentiful, and not revolve around anyone else's expectations, ridicule, or spectacle. For this reason, I love throuples and threesomes. I'm possibly happiest in the partnership of two people. And although I haven't engaged in that kind of communion much since the early days of my divorce, it was, for me, an essential part of understanding my sexual orientation.

For years I'd been called toward the divinely feminine, but now, I was finally seeking it.

In a 1984 interview with Richard Goldstein of *The Village Voice*, James Baldwin says, "There's nothing in me that is not in everybody else . . . I loved a few people and they loved me. It had nothing to do with these labels."

Still unlearning the binary loop of my past, where I could only be gay or straight, I originally looked at Baldwin's words as a place where he *hadn't* healed, a sign that he was still uncomfortable calling himself a gay Black man. Baldwin saying that he wasn't "into labels" seemed to be evidence of being a person of his time, which was filled with homophobia.

But it was only myself I was erasing from the personal history and narratives of James Baldwin by not recognizing the precision in his choice of "queer," as opposed to gay, as an identity. His novels *Giovanni's Room* and *Another Country* are rightly touted as gay cultural milestones: both clearly feature bisexual characters, and in the case of *Another Country*, characters are referred to as queer—male and female, Black and white. (This was in 1962, the same year Helen Gurley Brown was telling us in *Sex and the Single Girl* that the consensus of psychiatrists was that lesbian sex was "cuckoo.")

I wonder how Baldwin would write this new world, in which our language for identity has a widening spectrum. I'm excited to see space opening up in popular media for more of us to see ourselves reflected sexually and culturally, but it's also important to see where we came from—and how much girls like you and me have had to endure in order to become our truest selves. Sure, the *Seventeen* magazine from all those years ago didn't say that secret fantasies and lesbian leanings were bad—but it also didn't say they mattered, instead claiming they didn't carry any weight. This rhetoric kept me ignorant of myself for decades; I didn't—couldn't—see myself. And as long as my homo-, pan-, or bisexuality could be kept in the box of appreciation or fantasy, I could still be acceptable. Someone's good little girlfriend or wife.

This problem extended beyond me; it affected how I viewed my kindred people, too. My response to proud Black queer heroes like Suge Avery (and by extension her author, Alice Walker) was to retrofit their identities into the straight world. Suge Avery wasn't bi. She was a wild, loose woman who "appreciated the company" of both men and women. She and Celie weren't a couple, per se. They were women like the half dozen or so pairs I'd known among older family and friend groups who had been married or in long-term relationships with men in their younger years and since given up on the opposite sex. Women who were "just friends."

We have to stop doing this. We have to stop writing and rewriting the history of humanity to ascribe strangeness and marginality to those who love beyond a heteronormative status quo. Especially because so many of us have been pushed into a binary, told who we are by others, taught to ignore ourselves. Removing—no—*reinventing* these narratives of everything outside straightness as deviant or derivative is the only way future generations of women will be able to possess any kind of autonomy. Take it from me: a woman who's played both sides of the coin, from straight virgin to queer divorcée.

A world is emerging in which we have representation for

the parts of me, the parts of us, that were severely lacking in my girlhood. Like Daniel Levy's pansexual character David Rose on *Schitt's Creek*, who describes himself, like a Baldwin-inspired millennial, as being "into the wine and not the label"; Zendaya's Rue Bennett on *Euphoria*, who falls in love with her trans bestie; Amandla Stenberg, the teen-movie heartthrob who's openly gay in real life and doesn't have to hide behind a loaded spice rack, as Jonathan Taylor Thomas did, to be accepted as beautifully normal.

Shit, all of this is beautiful to me.

In Pursuit of Brown-on-Brown Love
Jennifer Chowdhury

After twenty years of chasing a
Bollywood-worthy story, I was exhausted.

The *Beverly Hills, 90210* collector's card featuring Jason Priestley (aka Brandon Walsh) slid out of my fourth-grade math textbook and straight into my mother's hands.

I got the tongue-lashing of my life.

She might've whooped me with her customary wooden spatula; I can't remember. What I recall most is being horrified that she'd discovered my crush. I wasn't allowed to watch *90210*, but sometimes I sneaked an episode or two. I'd traded a book with a classmate for the collector's card so I wouldn't be the only girl in my class without one.

My mom's eyes were on fire as she tossed Jason Priestley in the trash. I found it unfair that she was so angry about a silly celeb crush. He wasn't like, real, or anything. Besides, my sister and I had been obsessed with Bollywood movie star Salman Khan since I was four years old, and she poked fun at us for it all the time. She even indulged our obsession by buying costly English-language Indian entertainment magazines from Indian grocery stores in Jackson Heights, Queens. It was an absolute must for my sister and me to rent the latest Salman Khan flick as soon as it appeared on pirated cassettes.

Despite my mother's rhetoric against having unholy thoughts and boys being sinful, I realized the real problem was that Jason Priestley was white. A Bollywood crush was cute; an American heartthrob crush was worrisome, lest it give me the wrong ideas about falling in interracial love.

This was my first lesson in placing my own identity on a higher pedestal than the world told me to, a way of beating back white supremacy: no white boys allowed.

My parents are devout Muslims and consider it blasphemy to marry outside of the religion, and—because of cultural sentiments—outside of the race. Like so many first-generation immigrant parents, they were focused on making sure their American-born daughters were connected to their roots.

Their race consciousness, too, ran deep. As a new immigrant and mom of two in her early twenties, my mother devoured PBS documentaries and taught us everything she learned about racism, the history of colonization, and the effects of white supremacy. I learned early on that European settlers had stolen and looted this land from its indigenous inhabitants, then shipped in boatloads of African men, women, and children to work it, and eventually brought in more labor from other parts of the world, countries where people's skin was deeper, more complicated, more resilient.

"We deserve to be in America, which is stolen land," my mom would say. "But it doesn't mean we have to live the way white people live!" No way her daughters were lending any part of their bodies, and most certainly not their uteruses, to the white male.

Other people of color—aka anyone non-Bangladeshi—were also off-limits, especially if they weren't Muslim. (Eventually, my mother conceded—but only theoretically and begrudgingly—that Muslims of other communities were fair game as spouses.)

As a young adult, I started to adopt similar sentiments: "For hundreds of years, white men colonized my uterus," I would spout off to friends. I wasn't going to willingly subject myself to further colonization by procreating with a white guy. I was expected to marry one of my own, and truth be told, I was perfectly fine with that.

Skin tone and ethnicity weren't part of the body-image issues I struggled with, though there were others, intrinsic to being a girl and the first child of immigrant parents. I loved Brown skin and Brownness. It helped to grow up in New York City among various shades and complexions. I also loved being trilingual, speaking English, Bengali, and its close cousin Hindi, the language of Bollywood movies. These cultures also came with their own fashion and food and music. I didn't ever want to choose; instead, I tried to blend all these identities together however I could, to create a life that combined the best of all my worlds.

It also helped that I didn't grow up around a ton of white people. My Queens neighborhood was low and middle income, home to Latin, Greek, and South Asian immigrants. Not quite the hood, but adjacent, and so my taste in men always ran hood-adjacent, too. I owned the street-smart-boy-falls-in-love-with-book-smart-girl story pretty hard, but with a Bengali twist. I wanted my romantic trysts to be a perfect blend of Western life and Eastern sensibilities.

By the time I hit puberty, the South Asian diaspora had finally acquired street cred: Jay-Z had teamed up with Panjabi MC—a British Indian rapper—to produce a hit track that played nonstop on the radio and in clubs, further cementing my Brown pride instead of wishes for blond hair and blue eyes. In fact, where I grew up, whiteness bordered on corny; membership in the Black and Brown worlds carried with it grit and edge.

And so, I never once thought of American culture as being exclusively "white," even though the dominance of whiteness was difficult to deny.

Though I desired Brown love, I didn't want it the way my parents envisioned it. As a kid, my worst fear was having an arranged marriage like my parents; I was determined to find love on my own. My worries weren't unfounded: in the future, I'd spend my twenties and early thirties fending off what were known as biodatas, résumés of prospective grooms from the motherland, which were really just packets of awkwardly posed, horribly filtered photos of eligible men who had graduated from top schools around the world.

But my checklist did not include marrying a man from Bangladesh and bringing him back home with me. I'd always wanted my male counterpart to be a fellow kid of immigrants or someone who'd immigrated themselves at an early age. An unbridgeable gap of language and ideologies existed between men straight from the homeland and women like me.

It might be a cliché to assume that every South Asian person is affected by Bollywood—though it is the world's largest entertainment industry and 85 percent of the content is love stories. I'm sure my Brown kinfolk will roll their eyes at yet another Desi girl writing about it. But really, the twisted blend of misogyny and romance that Bollywood promotes, its free pronunciations of love and sexuality, are essential to so many South Asian immigrant kids. It's the only education on sex and romance we get.

In 1995, a movie came out that would change everything: *Dilwale Dulhania Le Jayenge*, loosely translated in mainstream Hindi to *Lover Will Take His Bride*. In a small town in Mumbai, that movie has been playing without pause since its release twenty-five years ago.

The protagonist is raised in London by working-class Indian parents (Hi! Fellow child of working-class Bangladeshis here!)—an extremely strict father who upholds cultural norms and a mother who secretly wants more freedom for her two daughters (I have a younger sister!) but raises her girls with as much cultural baggage as possible.

The opening scene introduces the heroine, Simran, in true, glorious '90s Bollywood fashion: she dances in her backyard wearing a white crop top and flouncy short skirt, thick and taut brown thighs swaying underneath, as she sings about meeting the man of her dreams—though she's technically promised in marriage to the son of a family friend who lives in India.

When a letter from her prospective in-laws arrives on her birthday, reality hits: her marriage will be for familial honor and ritual.

She asks her father for just a brief interlude of freedom: a monthlong trip around Europe with her friends. It's a big ask. She usually isn't allowed to go anywhere alone, much less travel internationally. But because she is an obedient daughter—and maybe because he knew doomsday was coming—her father lets her go.

In a London train station, Simran meets Raj, the prototype for straight male love interests of my generation: rich, Brown, utterly charming, and with hair to die for.

Also obnoxious and problematic as hell, but I wouldn't understand that for at least another fifteen years.

And yes, of course, by the end of the movie, Simran dramatically runs through another train station to catch her beloved before he leaves. In true Bollywood fashion, she ends up with Raj and is released from her promised match. True love always wins.

"Only your husband deserves your body." My mother was just one step short of tattooing this phrase onto my forehead when I was in middle school. The world's biggest threat wasn't a serial killer or a rapist, it was a Bangladeshi Muslim boy who would use me as practice and leave me for someone who didn't open up her legs (and also heart, I guess) that easily.

The threat was moot, because when the budding breasts and swelling asses of my female classmates were coming into their own, my flat-chested, frizzy-haired self was ignored, to say the least. The most popular and sought-after girls were Puerto Rican and Colombian. My first real-life crush was half and half, and his girlfriend was a slim Boricua with a set of bouncy boobs and butt to match.

All throughout middle school, I got no play—until the last semester of eighth grade, when one of my own, an older cousin's friend who was easily mistaken for one of the coveted Puerto Rican guys, came checkin' for me just as my body was finally beginning to emerge.

I was a shy fourteen-year-old, the class nerd—what did I know about love, boys, or relationships? M. went to the high school next door; taking a cue from my favorite Bollywood heroines, I clutched my books and pointedly ignored him. I enacted the part perfectly.

Of course, I was secretly thrilled that I'd caught the attention of a fly guy from my community. The Bangladeshi American circle is small and relatively new, only one to three generations old, and it was a rarity to find a straight male partner who had been raised in America like I had been.

How lucky was I? I hadn't even started high school and I'd already found my husband!

M.'s mating call was a particular Bollywood song he'd play as he drove down my block in his souped up Honda Civic hatchback. "Oh oh, jaane jaana, dhundhe tujhe deewana." In English, "Oh oh, my sweetheart, your crazy lover is looking for you." I'd run to my fire escape and secretly wave to him as he passed by. That one act of defiance felt like a triumph because I wasn't allowed to date. Not at fourteen, not ever. Either my parents were supposed to find me a husband, or I was magically supposed to meet an appropriate guy who checked off all their boxes and convince him on Day One to marry me.

Before long, M. grew bored of the good girl he'd bagged and dumped me for an older, sexier friend of his, and I experienced my first heartbreak.

For the next eighteen years, a series of boyfriends would follow, all different iterations of the same guy. Always a couple of years older than me (I'd been taught not to choose someone my age, since girls mature faster than boys). Always Bangladeshi, raised there until twelve or thirteen before spending his teens in America, so he could romance me with both R&B and Bollywood jams.

My second high school boyfriend controlled what I wore, what I ate, who I was friends with, and drove me to school and back. I turned sixteen, then seventeen, and wanted to break free. After several attempts to break up with him, I convinced him that I'd cheated on him so he'd end the relationship himself.

My college boyfriend told me I was too outspoken to become a part of his family. His mother was a controlling matriarch by his own admission and held up antiquated standards of patriarchy. She wanted a daughter-in-law who would submit to her and her son, and her approval was paramount for my ex. My body, he said, would also offend his mother. To him: curvy. To her: fat, a reminder of her son's pleasure principle. When I expressed my desire to be a foreign correspondent, he told me teaching was a good career choice for a Brown girl.

By graduation, I thought it was the perfect time to meet each other's parents and get engaged, but he straight-up told me what I'd been dreading to hear: I wasn't marriage material.

For Bangladeshi girls from conservative families, marriage was the only way to attain independence and freedom. We didn't go away to college or move to different cities on our own. We were expected to live in our fathers' homes until we got married. And as rebellious as I was, I also wanted to stay true to this narrative. It was a picture-perfect story: fall in love with a fellow Bangladeshi immigrant kid, have a big Bollywood-style wedding, blend our families together, and live happily ever after.

And so, in my midtwenties, I got engaged to a man whom I'd met while visiting family in Atlanta. A decade older than me, he had recently moved to Georgia from Bangladesh—an FOB (fresh off the boat), as Asian Americans often demeaningly call new immigrants. I had grown up using the term to distance myself from Bangladeshis who hadn't grown up in the United States as I had and thus establish my "superiority."

My new fiancé was charming and desperate to please me. For him, snagging me was an achievement, a move up the diaspora class ladder. That importance gave me a temporary high, until the misery of having virtually nothing in common—and, more importantly, not being in love with him—forced me to rethink things. I broke off the engagement.

It was time to try something different. If I wanted a home outside of my parents', it was time to get one for myself. Sans husband. Sans marriage. Sans a man.

Which was how I landed in San Francisco, six months after I broke off the engagement. Simple enough: new place, new life, lived on my own terms. But letting go of a dream I'd cultivated since I was a child was harder than I'd imagined. It was tough to enjoy my independence when I hadn't yet gained emotional autonomy.

In California, I was the most single I'd ever been. At twenty-seven, the pressure to find someone was looming, especially the pressure from my parents, who thought I was wasting away my life going out with friends and traveling. They hadn't approved of my ex-fiancé, social class differences being their main objection, so they were relieved I wasn't marrying him. But our split made them more eager to see me married to their idea of the right person.

I'm convinced that the universe conspired for me to meet the next (and—spoiler alert—last) in the series of toxic men in my life.

I practically cartwheeled toward A.; I thought this was finally my chance to find the kind of partner I kept missing the mark on. He was a Bangladeshi American kid from New Jersey with both hip-hop and Bollywood references to prove it. He, at last, was going to make me wifey.

I moved back to New York for him, and throughout the four years of our relationship he disappeared every three months. He would change his number and delete his social media accounts, and I waited, taking him at his word when he showed up again and attributed these absences to depression. A good partner was supportive. I would endure anything, even repeated abandonment.

The last straw wasn't even when he got engaged to another woman. Or when he slapped, punched, kicked, and dragged me across the floor, holding scissors over my face and threatening to gouge my eyes out. The impetus to finally break free from this toxicity came when I lost a job I loved and had worked years to get, couldn't pay rent on my dream apartment, and had to move back in with my parents. My independent life—which I wasn't supposed to have had in the first place, which none of my female ancestors had ever had—crumbled. Everything I'd built for myself was gone.

And so was the dream I'd destroyed it for.

After twenty years of chasing a Bollywood-worthy story, I was exhausted. It was time to do things differently. To stop dating for a while and learn to enjoy my own company. To accept that life without a traditional marriage to a man with a superficial list of qualities was the healthier choice. The narrative I'd been fed as a girl about what Brown-on-Brown love would look like might've worked out for the other Bangladeshi girls I grew up with, but I started to think—peacefully—that my path was meant to veer away from this narrative.

Three years of working through the fear of loneliness to discover the unimaginable perks and freedom of singlehood led to the opportunity to achieve another dream: a foreign correspondent position in Bangladesh covering the Rohingya refugee crisis. The move also provided me space to take the pressure off getting married and healthily distance myself from my family and the close-knit immigrant community I grew up in. It was too painful to continue my patterns and live in the world I'd known my whole life.

And, reader, as you probably predicted: that's when I finally met my husband.

I had no clue I was starting a whole new chapter of my love life when a new friend and her boyfriend invited me on a trip to the scenic Chittagong Hill Tracts of southern Bangladesh, where foreigners usually aren't allowed. Some of her boyfriend's friends joined us, and one of them chatted me up. He poured me drink after drink, carried my luggage off the bus to the hotel, rolled joints for me. I was living on the edge of homesickness, and he felt like home.

We became inseparable. And every day I thought, *This is temporary. This could never work.* I was five years older than him, we had no shared intellectual pursuits, and he was *from* Bangladesh. My God, the irony and shame of marrying him. Only desperate women went back to the motherland to get married.

But he never asked about my dating history, criticized my body, or judged my career. He was proud of dating one of just a handful of Bangladeshi American women journalists in the world. Lesser things had unhinged my exes, most of whom never left their neighborhoods in the tristate area. I'd since realized that those men had to sink me because they never felt they could measure up. They loved my freewheeling nature, the pride I took in all aspects of my identity; I was down with the culture *and* down at the club. But when it came time to marry, only one part of my multifaceted identity fit the centuries-old patriarchal standards for choosing a wife.

My time living in Bangladesh, traveling extensively across Asia, and falling in love with someone from outside my world taught me that I had a lot of internalized racism to undo. I'd learned early on to push back against white supremacy, but I had subconsciously aligned myself with whiteness by placing myself above certain categories of immigrants and people like my husband.

Once I let go of expectations of who I was supposed to end up with, I fell in love with my husband as a whole person and not just because of our ethnic ties. That was the piece of the puzzle in my quest for love that I'd been missing. For two decades, I'd carried around a mental checklist—as most of us do—and never deviated from it. It's important to know what you want in a partner, but it can't be the North Star.

We're married now, with a daughter, living in New York City. I fretted about him adjusting to a new country, a new culture, but he carries his core self with him no matter where he is. He also ensures that I never lose myself in him, in our marriage, or even in our daughter.

Despite sharing a language and cultural background, we've had completely different life experiences. We didn't need to go through the same trauma to learn from each other, to respect each other's thoughts and desires. He helped me find what I truly craved and identify what had been there all along: an unwavering sense of self.

IVF and the Single Girl
Evette Dionne

I've learned over the years that there's
nothing lonely about being single.

Being thirty-two and single was never part of the plan. In fact, I'd
been socialized to believe—and bought deeply into the idea—that
my life trajectory would follow a path I knew well from popular
culture: I'd graduate from college, get another degree if it suited
me, begin building my career in a fulfilling field, stumble into a
meet-cute, get married two years later, purchase a home, have a
child or maybe two, and spend the remainder of my life juggling
my needs and wants with those of my family.

Few of those milestones were in the cards for me.

I've been single since 2018. After spending four years with the
person I assumed I'd stay with, I decided I'd rather be alone than
push down dissatisfaction and unhappiness in order to preserve
the façade of perfection. Everything changed when I relocated to
New York—alone—for my dream job in digital editing. Though my
then partner and I had planned for him to come to New York once
I'd found an apartment and settled in, over time, my confidence
grew in my ability to independently create a life for myself.

In my new reality, I was responsible only for myself: I sublet a studio apartment, complete with the brick accent wall I'd always wanted. I paid the rent alone. Night after night, I cooked or ordered dinner for one. I made new friends, many of whom were single or in long-distance relationships, and we frequented happy hours together. I didn't feel a need to rush home by a certain time to accommodate a partner's wants or expectations. I dirtied every dish in my cabinet. All the clothes in the hamper, waiting to be washed, belonged to me. I decorated without worrying about leaving space for another person's flair.

In short, through this process of separating from my partner, something miraculous happened. I felt as though I were walking through a mansion with an endless number of doors, all of which were open: I was excelling at work, I'd landed a literary agent and begun crafting a book proposal, and I had much more free time to figure out what actually brought me joy. Instead of shaping my preferences around someone else's, I could dictate where I lived, if and when I cooked, what time I came home, and how I spent my evenings.

As I became more comfortable being away from my partner, I also became more content being alone. Inevitably, we drifted apart and decided to end our relationship altogether. But though I'd chosen to be uncoupled, a part of me felt it was just "for now." I still harbored a secret desire to eventually live out the rom-com I'd been sold. I'd meet the man—one who's intelligent, loving, unintimidated by my career goals because he's similarly ambitious, understanding about my need for space, someone with whom I could share inside jokes and routines. I imagined the perfect balance between being a magazine editor and author, a present partner and parent.

It hadn't yet come true, but wouldn't it?

As I got older, I wondered if I should once and for all stop waiting for the moment when the person—my person—showed up. Ultimately, life made that decision for me.

After being diagnosed with left-ventricle heart failure at twenty-nine and then developing pulmonary hypertension, a progressive lung condition, at thirty, I could no longer wait for the "right" person to decide how—or if—I'd create a family. And when my cardiologist told me that pregnancy was now a contraindicated condition for me—meaning there's a 50 percent chance I'd die, my baby would die, or we'd both die—it knocked the breath out of me. I was no longer on a fictional timeline; I could no longer wait idly by for my Hollywood meet-cute. When I was prescribed a pulmonary hypertension medication that causes severe birth defects, I knew I needed to retrieve my eggs before it was no longer an option for me to share DNA with a potential child. Egg retrieval is the first step in the long process of IVF; eventually, I could choose to have the eggs fertilized and attempt implantation through a surrogacy arrangement.

Within twenty-four hours, I decided to embark on the arduous journey of egg retrieval and IVF, husband be damned. I contacted a fertility doctor, made an appointment, tweeted about my intentions to give myself an extra layer of accountability, and plunged headfirst into the process.

It took twelve weeks from the moment I made that decision until the moment I woke up in the recovery room after having my eggs retrieved—and it was the longest twelve weeks of my entire life. Infertility clinics often presume that those seeking their services are doing so with a partner after having difficulty conceiving. This is sometimes the case, but there's now a growing subset of people, myself included, who freeze their eggs for later use—with or without someone else in the picture. According to a 2018 article in *The New York Times*, more than twenty thousand women in the United States have frozen their eggs, though there's less concrete data about how many of those procedures have since resulted in live births.

Even the paperwork reinforces the assumption that most women are undergoing the procedure with a partner. An entire section requests information about a spouse, presumably one who's cisgender and heterosexual: What's his name? His birth date? Has his sperm been tested? Are there genetic disorders within his family history? Does he consent to his partner exploring IVF?

As I completed these forms in November 2020, mere weeks after I'd decided that IVF was the best route for me to create the family I desired, I expected it to be a breeze. Instead, it sat heavily on my chest, as if all the work I'd done to make myself comfortable being single might be undone. I began questioning: *Could* I be a single parent?

As I attempted to grapple with those feelings, I returned, once again, to Glynnis MacNicol's memoir *No One Tells You This*, which was essential in bringing the beauty of singlehood into focus for me. She chronicles her life as a forty-year-old writer living in New York City, navigating her mother's terminal Parkinson's diagnosis and figuring out how to exist without the husband and child that society tells her she should want. "[I]t was a truth universally acknowledged that by age forty I was supposed to have a certain kind of life, one that, whatever else it might involve, included a partner and babies," she writes. "If this story wasn't going to end with a marriage or a child, what then? Could it even be called a story?"

If my own story didn't include a partner, I wondered, was it still worth telling?

I asked myself this question as I skipped over the portion of the paperwork about my presumed partner's medical history, and again as I ventured to the clinic alone, day in and day out, to be poked with phlebotomy needles that tested my estrogen levels and prodded with vaginal ultrasound wands that measured the size of my uterine lining and my eggs. I asked myself again as I cried in my car because I'd been told that my eggs weren't big enough to be retrieved, meaning I needed another two days of hormone injections in my already bruised abdomen, and as I watched my savings account dwindle as the literal cost increased. The question reverberated as sharply as the pain from the worst uterine cramps I'd ever experienced when I woke up alone in the recovery room.

There's so much to know about IVF, and it's a steep learning curve, especially for folks, myself included, navigating it without the support of a partner, health insurance, or a patient advocate. It was just me and my village: my parents, one of whom injected me in the abdomen with hormones twice a day for thirteen days; my friends, who checked in on me every moment, sent gift cards, and helped me make peace with my sudden mood swings; and my coworkers, who didn't bat an eyelash at the long hours I spent at the fertility clinic.

That's what singlehood has provided me: an opportunity to create the family I desire instead of the one society has prescribed to me.

I've learned over the years that there's nothing lonely about being single. When my family dog died a few months before my egg retrieval, my friends sent flowers, cards, and even a frame for my favorite picture of her. When I had a myomectomy to extract five fibroids from my abdomen, my parents and friends rallied around me, from helping me shower and sit up to comforting me through the recovery pain. Rather than relying on a primary romantic partner to be everything—to orient my life around—I have the power, the fortitude, and the agency to create the village I need and deserve.

Between appointments, medications, the procedure itself, and storage, egg freezing cost me a little more than thirteen thousand dollars. It will cost me nearly double that and possibly more to birth my child through a surrogate. That doesn't even begin to account for how much it will cost to raise that child, most likely without a partner, or how much it will cost to repeat the process if I decide to have a second.

Then again, time is elusive, especially for people like me with chronic illness. There's no telling if today is the today your condition takes a turn for the worse. And while I still spend many nights anxious about what the next day will bring, there's one worry I'm not troubled by at all: motherhood. I know it will happen in its time because I've alleviated the pressure of my "biological clock." My eggs are forever thirty-one, so no matter when they're implanted in a surrogate—next week, next month, five years from now—I'll be able to become a mother on my terms and in my time. I can live my life uncoupled for as long as I'd like. I can travel, I can switch jobs, I can remain nomadic or purchase a home.

My story of starting IVF is one I would relive over and over again if I had to. It's how I found out that being single isn't the end; in fact, it's often just the beginning.

Thank U, Ex
Rosemary Donahue

Often, marriage is presented not just as a revered
institution but as a worthy pursuit—*a goal*—so
to choose divorce is to choose failure.

Thanksgiving 2015–2016

Dane and I have a history of contracted timelines. We first connected through comments on mutual friends' Facebook posts. After a few days of rapid-fire messaging, we exchanged numbers and
started texting or FaceTiming for the better part of each day. Three
months passed, and I booked a ticket to JFK. Within days, our individual visions for the future came into focus, and he decided to put
his life in a storage unit to come live with me and my dog, Milo, in
Southern California for the summer, after which we'd move back to
Brooklyn together. Though in hindsight a big jump like this could
have been a disaster, we loved living together and left for the East
Coast as planned. After six days driving across the country, mostly
staying at campgrounds in a small tent I'd bought years before, we
finally opened the door to an apartment that was truly ours. Within
a month, we'd adopted another dog, Lily, and six months later we
decided, over text, to get married.

My family, both immediate and extended, loved Dane. My parents aren't very traditional and had never put any pressure, implicit or explicit, on me to partner or have children. However, they liked who Dane was as an individual and who I was around him.

When he met my extended family in Cherry Hill, New Jersey, it seemed they felt similarly. Some of them are Jewish, some Christian, and others aren't really anything at all, so we typically split the difference and celebrate the holiday season on Thanksgiving (a day with its own set of problems). We gather over turkey, my grandmother's pumpkin chiffon pie, and my aunt's kugel. This annual tradition became Dane's, too; he grew close with the entire, sprawling crew in our first two years together.

But planning our nuptials was stressful, as we both navigated the uncertainty of looking for jobs, the election and inauguration of Trump, and what I now realize was increasing tension before my inevitable coming out as queer. Perhaps it would have been kinder, easier, less expensive to call off the wedding then, but I've had to learn a lot of things the hard way.

Maybe that's why I still went through with the wedding even after I told everyone that I was queer, why I said I didn't need to know more about this side of myself first or to experiment with my sexuality, and why I continued to chalk up my yearslong depression and low libido to ineffective medication and severe trauma. Maybe it's also why I popped a Xanax before I walked down the aisle hand in hand with Dane in front of our family and friends, or why the first drink I'd had in over a year was on my wedding night. Acknowledging the story of my queerness meant reframing the story of Dane and me as the romantic loves of each other's lives—and I wasn't ready to do that yet.

The thing is, I tend to let myself get pushed all the way to the edge before making a necessary leap, even if someone else is out there hanging on for dear life beside me. It's hard for me to pause, reconsider, and change course, because I've learned to repress my needs as a survival tactic. It's only when it becomes so urgent that a manual override of that system is necessary—when something within me wakes up, sweaty and screaming from a nightmare— that I'm able to finally make the jump.

Thanksgiving 2017

I don't remember much about it; one of my two married Thanks-givings.

Thanksgiving 2018

I burst into tears during our weekly couples therapy session with such an uncharacteristic loss of control that I shocked both my husband and our therapist. Dane had been filling in John—who always wore a patterned, short-sleeved button-up with a contrast-ing bow tie—on his recent work trip to Austin, and all of a sudden there I was, blubbering on the couch and saying something in-cluding the phrases "open marriage" and "my sexuality." John looked at me with concern, and I realized that I needed to slow down. I grabbed a few tissues, sopped up the mascara stream-ing down my face, took a breath, and started over. I told them I felt as though being out as queer in theory but not practice wasn't enough for me; I was worried that the longer I went without dating other queer people, the more I'd resent myself for never trying. I needed to date—and eventually have sex with—people other than cis men.

While he was always a wonderful therapist, John couldn't hide his bald-faced shock at the turn the last forty-five minutes had taken. As we left the room, he urged us to take it easy for the next week and think about how we wanted things to look in the future, rather than acting on anything right away. And, of course, like the good gay therapist he was, he suggested we read both *The Ethical Slut* and *Opening Up*, but not before warning us of the books' heteronormative language.

Over the next few days, Dane and I began to discuss the vague outlines of this new thing we were about to try. Were acquaintances off the table? Would we use Tinder? What other questions *should* we be asking ourselves?

We told my parents about our new arrangement prior to my family's annual holiday dinner so they'd be sensitive to shifts in our dynamic. While they presented a supportive front, they later revealed they were worried we might not make it. Still, they helped us dodge well-meaning but slightly invasive questions from relatives about a future that now had a giant question mark over it. We left New Jersey right after dessert.

During our next therapy session, we discussed the rules for our open relationship. Dane went on a date that week and felt optimistic about the possibilities of nonmonogamy for us; I went on a date and quickly knew that our marriage needed to end, for his sake as much as for mine. Within three days, I found my own apartment, packed up my things, and moved out. A whirlwind ending equal to our love story.

Thanksgiving 2019

It was going to be my first time seeing everyone since the divorce had gone through in May, though my brother—a trusted buffer for all things familial—was staying behind in California with his girlfriend. While my parents and extended family lean more progressive than not, I'd been feeling more protective of myself since I came out. Strangely enough, it seemed Dane was, too.

"I'll go with you, if you want," he texted me as I sat on the floor of my apartment, petting Milo and staring off into the distance.

After a minute or so, I typed out a response: "Thank you, that's so sweet. Ultimately, I think that would confuse them all even more. I'll just skip it this year."

If you'd told me back in, say, April of that year that Dane and I would be talking at all—let alone that he would be offering to make the annual family trip to Jersey with me—I might have burst out laughing. I knew it was unusual to be so close again after any breakup, let alone a divorce; then again, it was never our style to follow typical timelines.

So, even though I decided to forgo the big gathering, Dane and I still spent Thanksgiving together. We holed up with some terrible TV, ordered Chinese food, and watched our dogs—which we still share—play together in my tiny living room. He posted a photo of us on Twitter, joking, "Almost a year since @rosadona broke up with me #thankful."

While I try to be discerning about the information I share online, I do tend to talk about parts of my personal life—whether experiences with sexual assault or mental health or relationships—in that space. Over the years, I've had many people say, both in public replies and private DMs, that my words have helped them.

As Dane and I found our way back to friendship and reinvented what our postdivorce relationship might look like, we began to share our process online and found that many others our age were going through similar transitions. Our tiny, 280-character stories would be retweeted with phrases like "divorce goals," and though internet-speak can make me cringe when applied to deeper matters, it was heartening to see our experience resonate with others. There were people in our DMs who were getting divorced and wanted to stay friends with their exes but weren't sure how to navigate the process. Others had been repressing parts of themselves for years and wanted to feel less alone as they disclosed these truths. Others still were dealing with the heartbreak of suddenly being left. Though the most common narrative attached to divorce is the tired story of a broken home, many people are looking for a blueprint that proves something better can be built in the aftermath.

Then again, we were also accused of desecrating the sanctity of marriage (isn't a little trolling a sign you're doing something right?). Often, marriage is presented not just as a revered institution but as a worthy pursuit—*a goal*—so to choose divorce is to choose failure. To call it quits is to eschew the traditional family structures we've been told uphold society. In many ways, it's seen as selfish to get divorced, and most of us have learned that selfishness is ugly, a major transgression.

I firmly believe that, for the most part, people don't opt out of a marriage unless they need to, and almost all divorces—even those most painful for one party or both—are necessary and good. After all, even if someone else makes the choice for you, isn't it the right decision, in the end, if it leaves you open to a love that's reciprocal?

Thanksgiving 2020

In the city where we live just a block apart, Dane and I walked our dogs together and talked about how we were dealing with the isolation of the pandemic. He told me about his girlfriend, and I talked to him about what it was like to try to date while COVID-19 was at the forefront of everyone's minds. It felt natural as anything, and it was. We've been through so many iterations of what a relationship can be, and we're still standing. I no longer call him the love of my life—in fact, I'm no longer sure I believe in that concept at all. I've settled on calling him "*a* love of my life." And now, without the pressure of "forever" hanging over our heads, it actually feels more likely that we'll be in each other's lives for a really long time.

Party of One
Josie Pickens

> Though it's taken more than twenty years,
> I'm finally done obsessing over belonging
> to others. . . . I practice polyamory.

My friend Abby just turned thirty and is feeling the itch to be a wife and mother. Given my ripe old age of forty-four, she looks to me for guidance on how to navigate that longing. I must know, she believes, since I'm the doting mother of a sweet and quirky fifteen-year-old; I've also been married twice and engaged five times (which seems outrageous now that I see it written).

Luckily for Abby, I've reached a point in my life where I'm not interested in pretending that I've ever shared her deep desire to be someone's everything. Instead, I tell her that being a wife is not all it's cracked up to be, that the system of heteropatriarchy insists she'll always be expected to give more than she receives. I tell her that I often agreed to marriage because I was in love—and because I hadn't been able to imagine feeling that way about someone and *not* wanting to be their wife.

All the women I knew growing up (including my mother, who married at eighteen) wed early in their lives. I understand why.

Many of them—especially the Black women who reached adulthood in the 1950s and '60s—viewed marriage as an opportunity for stability and safety, and even sometimes as a way out. In 1965, when my mother married, it would've been difficult to purchase a home, rent an apartment, or even buy a car without a man's approval and cosignature.

My mother needed to marry if she was going to leave my grandparents' farm in southwest Louisiana and the small parish where she was born, so in some ways, she viewed marriage as a path toward freedom. And it certainly offered her more independence than my grandmother had ever known: for starters, she birthed just three children to my grandmother's eleven. This meant that my mother could spend *some* time exploring who she was outside of her roles as wife and caretaker. She was able to live in an urban, progressive city where she could work at a boutique bakery and learn cake design, instead of committing to a life of farming or "homemaking."

For many of the women from my mother's generation, saying "I do" also meant they were all grown up, that life had truly begun. And for a long time, I held on to my mother's definition of marriage and what it meant to be fully grown, rather than exploring what both those things meant to me.

By my twenties, I'd accomplished a great deal. I had been an excellent student, a blossoming writer who'd transitioned well into the workforce. I could provide fully for myself, and I enjoyed being single and childless—very much. I took lovers, and left them, as I saw fit. I wasn't interested in defining relationships through antiquated social constructs. I much preferred allowing my love stories to write themselves. I never wanted to feel possessive toward someone else, and I ran fast in the other direction if I felt that a lover might be too possessive toward me.

I wasn't lonely. My bed was always filled with books, and when I wasn't out frolicking and being free, it was my sanctuary and favorite place to be. I had no real-time constraints and few responsibilities outside of those I'd taken on for myself. I cleaned and straightened up my home when I wanted and prepared elaborate meals for one every Sunday.

I had no idea how marvelous my life was then, though, because even in all my single-woman bliss, I still focused on some made-up future with a man I hadn't even met yet. Too much of my identity and my ideas around my worthiness were wrapped up in whether I would be chosen as a wife, and I didn't have any models for what life might look like if I continued to choose myself.

Now, though it's taken more than twenty years, I'm finally done obsessing over belonging to others. Instead, I'm committing to belonging deeply to myself, in the enchanting words of the Somali British poet Warsan Shire. I practice polyamory.

The realization that this lifestyle is what works best for me came during a therapy session when I talked about my longest and happiest relationship, which lasted almost a decade. With that partner, I broke away from many of my traditional patterns. He insisted on establishing a long friendship before we began dating exclusively, and focusing on that friendship made our connection stronger. It also alleviated a lot of pressure for both of us, as there was no rush to claim or possess one another. We dated other people while figuring out the terms of our connection. We also communicated *a lot* about our needs as they shifted and changed, and we "took breaks" when necessary—which freed up space for honesty, curiosity, and exploration.

Of course, there are numerous ways to practice polyamory. Some poly relationships are based in relationship anarchy, in which people operate in complete freedom and see all relationships as equal. Others are hierarchical and centered around a primary relationship, which can include marriage or other long-term connections. Additionally, someone can be sexually monogamous while practicing polyamory, but open to dating or having intimate and romantic ties with others. Or someone can have different sexual partners while also choosing to be monogamous when it comes to emotional intimacy.

And then there's me.

I am committed to myself, first and foremost. Any negotiations I make in relationships come as a result of making sure that my needs are being centered, valued, and met. After those essential steps are taken, I can be vulnerable and open to giving the love and care I receive—because I'm not pouring from an empty cup.

For many years, and after many failed romantic relationships, I thought my lack of desire for monogamy meant that I was broken. What I realize now is that I've always been polyamorous.

In the past, the nonmonogamy I practiced usually looked like serial monogamy: I would be fully rooted in and committed to a relationship for six months to a year before feeling a strong urge to be single again. Partnerships like these allowed me to meet societal expectations for women to be committed and "true" to one person, while the sense of freedom I acquired after a breakup satisfied my need for independence. But now, I've learned to be more transparent and ethical in the ways I communicate and address my needs for space to explore. It's a lot to ask of someone, that they belong to you and only you.

I would be disingenuous if I didn't admit that I bring some biases to my position on monogamy. My therapist believes that infidelity may be a trigger for me, and I don't deny that this is a factor in my feelings. I've seen the way cheating has destroyed people and families that I love; I've certainly felt its hard gut punch myself.

Still, why make promises (or demand promises) that so few of us are able to sustain?

For me, it's more than a jaded, unhealed heart determined not to hurt again. I also believe in vulnerability. I crave intimacy and understand that connection is a human need. I realize that finding and maintaining love requires risk-taking and work. And I continue to be open to it, believing it to be one of life's sweetest and wildest adventures. In fact, I've committed my life to helping myself and others become better lovers—to ourselves, to our romantic partners, to our families, and to our communities—through my writing and by curating public conversations.

This path toward choosing myself as my primary connection and focus began, in the words of the remarkable poet Audre Lorde, with "defining myself for myself." I needed to declare my own definitions of joy, love, care, and safety. I wanted to learn to enjoy my own company, deeply, which includes honoring and exploring my body through the ritual of self-pleasure.

To be clear, humans don't practice self-pleasure only through masturbation. Self-pleasure and self-care are inextricably linked. For me, practicing self-pleasure can look like expanding my daily yoga session or taking myself out on a date. It can also look like setting boundaries around tasks and people who might make me less joyful and less at peace.

But self-pleasure also includes loving (and loving on) my flesh. I started experiencing self-pleasure through masturbation long before I began having partnered sex. I still remember my first orgasm—the way my body quivered and my amazement over having made that sensation happen. From all I'd read and seen until that point, orgasms had to be given to women by men, and discovering that I didn't have to depend on anyone else to get off was empowering. I was unknowingly teaching myself sexual autonomy and that I'm responsible for navigating my own pleasure. Partners were a fine addition, but they were never mandatory.

I still bring this same energy into all my sexual experiences, but I've learned that it is also valuable to own and center my pleasure in every other aspect of my life. It's taking the time to rub my entire body with fragrant oil after I shower. It's staring at that same body in a full-length mirror and challenging myself to see what is beautiful about it instead of what I'd like to change. Self-pleasure is affirmation through touch and exploration, through finding the limbs that tingle with hunger for attention. I'm an expert on my own terrain; I'm more than satisfied with being a party of one.

As I become more comfortable moving about the world this way, what has been a huge surprise to me is how much space it's opened up for me to enjoy my relationships with others.

Part of my self-care and self-pleasure rituals involve taking an active role in my own healing, which means that I don't overly rely on my friends to play counselor (especially since many of them are also Black women who are grappling with racism, sexism, queer-antagonism, and so many other terrifying and depleting forms of violence). It took one of my best friends, Toni, bringing my habit of emotional dumping to my attention to make me understand that it was an issue. Instead of allowing our friendship to be strained or broken, Toni chose to be transparent with me. Not only did my friend express that she didn't have the emotional capacity to navigate the struggles she was facing in her life as well as the struggles I was facing in mine, she also reminded me that she was not a licensed therapist and that I deserved professional mental and emotional care. She was absolutely right.

I immediately reconnected with my therapist after that tough conversation, and that work allowed me to reenter my relationship with Toni (and my other friends) in a way that the topic of our conversations didn't always revolve around my personal struggles. We were able to return to interactions that centered joy.

I've also committed to bringing womanism—an ideology close to feminism that centers the experiences of Black women—into my mothering, especially as a single mom and primary caregiver. I speak openly with my daughter about who I am outside of being a parent; sometimes those conversations communicate my needs for alone time, for nights out with friends, and for travel with people I'm dating or partnered with.

Though I've been mothering for a decade and a half, it's still hard to navigate the shame I've internalized by prioritizing my needs and desires foremost. As women, we're taught that our children should come first in our lives—and if they don't, we're bad parents. But what I've found is that I'm a *better* mother when I make time for my own dreams and desires; it even helps me guide my daughter toward hers.

And I owe that work—of holding on to me—to my daughter as much as to myself. I hope that through communicating my autonomy, my daughter will be able to establish her own ways of developing personal sovereignty.

It might seem strange, egotistical even, to hear a woman speak about the importance of prioritizing herself before anyone else in relationships—even though men have practiced this behavior since the beginning of time.

Potential partners usually react to my decision to be poly and in a primary relationship with myself in one of two ways. They either become intent on changing my mind about nonmonogamy (and become quite angry when they can't), or they attempt to manipulate me into believing there's something unnatural, even shameful, about not wanting to commit to a long-term relationship or marriage.

What I've also learned, though, is that other people are open to letting go of old ideas about love and about how we—as humans—can exist in relationships, people who can be imaginative about sex and connection and care and all their glorious possibilities. I gravitate toward those people, who embody the words of poet Nikki Giovanni:

> show me someone not full of herself
> and i'll show you a hungry person.

I never want to be hungry again, and I'm not interested in connecting with anyone who prefers me that way. Sometimes I'm pleasantly surprised that I can connect with romantic partners who don't try to shame or change me—a Black, queer, polyamorous woman who chooses to make her needs and desires paramount. I've only started showing up to relationships as my full self in my forties. One of the joys of aging has been realizing that the world will make space for me, if I'm bold enough to be authentic.

I'm currently two years into a romantic relationship that amazes me every day. Iya and I check in with each other regularly to determine whether we feel safe and loved in our partnership. We ask each other if there is a need for more connection, or less, if there are spaces in our relationship that lack care, if we are interested in seeing other people. We commit, over and over, to not projecting or internalizing the answers to these questions. We choose to be grateful that we are both in places in our lives where these kinds of conversations don't make either of us feel ashamed or like the love we want to experience is impossible. I'm still in a primary relationship with myself, and Iya reinforces my right to prioritize my needs. In many ways, this is the relationship I've been dreaming of my entire life.

And so, when my friend Abby comes to me with those big questions about marriage and monogamy, I can say that I'm sure about what love looks like now, because I've learned to give myself the devotion that I once spent so much of my life giving to others.

In fact, I tell her, I'm always finding love.

Confessions of a Lonely Feminist
Nichole Perkins

I know I don't *need* a man to survive,
but I must admit I want one.

One day, Mama showed me a ring she'd bought herself. It was gold with a delicate display of diamonds, but bright and bold all the same.

"It's nice when a man buys things for you, but it's even better when you can buy them for yourself," she said. Despite my teenage impulse to ignore her, I paid attention.

Mama dropped this kind of advice in my lap, and yet she also told me the kind of man to look for—rich. And not because of a gold-digger mentality; it was so I wouldn't have to work as hard as she did. My mother worked as a nurse from sunup to sundown, and somehow we still qualified for food stamps, reduced lunches, and educational programs that encouraged Black kids from disadvantaged backgrounds to go to college.

As much as Mama stressed the need for a partner who could provide, she also emphasized to her kids—specifically the girls—that we should always have our own backs. We should never feel compelled to do something we didn't want to for the sake of a man. I absorbed these ideas completely, even as I secretly hatched a plan for myself: marry by twenty-six (right after completing my doctorate), then wrap up birthing children by thirty-three.

Despite the values she was instilling in us, Mama would never call herself a feminist. Once, vibrating with new knowledge gleaned from all the Black feminist texts I was reading in college, I told Mama she was the first feminist I ever knew. She bugged her eyes at me as if I'd just called her out her name. For many members of my mom's generation, especially Black women, feminism is a dirty word, equivalent to "man-hating." There's no empowerment in the term.

I'd only meant to acknowledge the way she maintained her independence, even as a working-class single mother. After my parents' divorce, she raised my sister, brother, and me on her own. She kept her dating life discreet, not wanting to bring home any men who weren't serious about her, but also hoping to set an example of not letting just any man come around. She was protecting us as much as herself. She wanted us to learn that people had to prove themselves to gain access to our lives.

In the early phase of my own love life, from ages fifteen to twenty-two, I had three long-term relationships, the last of which ended after college. A year after that breakup, I dropped out of graduate school and entered my "ho phase," with extended rounds of casual dating and hookups to make up for all the time I'd tried to play wife. Shaking off the cobwebs of monogamy, I entertained two-month stands and friends with benefits, exerting my feminist right to a "hit it and quit it" lifestyle that only men seemed to get away with. It was fun and mostly satisfying, and I learned a lot about myself, like what I will and won't tolerate from partners, no matter how temporary they might be.

After a while, though, I found myself longing for the warm rush of exclusive companionship.

Though I started dating more seriously and becoming involved in relationships that started out well enough but ended in pain and confusion, it's now been over ten years since my last commitment. Sure, I've had plenty of "situationships," those uncategorized trysts in which you do everything a monogamous couple does except tell each other how you feel, and the other person ends up gone anyway.

Sometimes the loneliness swells inside me so much, I wonder if I'll actually start floating through the clouds of weed smoke I exhale during those particularly rough moments. But then the high makes me horny, and I scroll through my phone, trying to find someone to take the edge off, before tossing it away. I can't be my full self with any of the options in my contact list; I'm never as soft and caring as I really am because I don't want them to mistake human decency for *feelings*. It's not that I'm lying; I simply don't enjoy being misunderstood—and too often, men think far too highly of themselves. I don't want a scrub thinking I've fallen for him just because I asked about his day. The idea that a guy with the world's most boring conversation but the world's most hearty dick might think I'm crushing on him almost sends me into a panic attack. Like the time I asked a guy if he wanted to meet for a drink before he came over, and he made sure to tell me he wasn't looking for anything serious.

Dude, it's a drink. I want a change of scenery and a reason to put on eyeliner, not a ring.

I'm over forty now, and I've learned to make it through life without serious, romantic love, or even a friend with benefits I can also call to help me move furniture. I know I don't *need* a man to survive, but I must admit I want one. I want someone I can hold hands with as we take too long in IKEA; I want to end my night with a forehead kiss pressing the words *I love you* into my skin; I want to wake up in the morning to the smell of a good breakfast some-one else has fixed just the way I like it. Oatmeal, thick. Bacon, oven baked and crispy soft. Biscuits with strawberry preserves. Orange juice, no pulp.

The loneliness pulls at me, and I feel ashamed, like I've aban-doned my mother's most important lesson: that I can take care of myself.

Yet sometimes—when I'm taking out the garbage for the thou-sandth time, or my unpaid freelance invoices are stacking up alongside bills with escalating late fees—I want to throw myself across the railroad tracks of my despair and wait to be rescued.

The COVID-19 pandemic didn't help matters. I live alone with my cat, Calliope, who I adopted in the midst of lockdown blues. Before all this, my professional life was finally matching my dreams: I had multiple book contracts and was cohosting an amazing podcast about pop culture and desire. Being a freelance writer wasn't exactly the stress-free, six-figure career Mama prayed I'd have, but I was finally doing what I loved. I had a great apartment in Brooklyn after years of subleases and couch surf-ing. I was in therapy and finally getting treatment for the major clinical depression that had been with me, untreated, since I was a child.

Still, there's only so much companionship a cat can provide. By midsummer, I took a chance on a couple of guys with strict pandemic protocols and went on some dates. We met at bars that served drinks outside, always within walking distance from my place, and if he passed the vibe check, we strolled back to my building—him nervous I might change my mind, me hoping he gave good head.

I rarely let anyone spend the night, and after each hookup left my apartment, I felt empty. It's true that when I decided to date again I wasn't looking for anything more meaningful. None of these men were my type or even all that interesting, but my body has needs.

Still, after I peed and washed up (always pee before and after sex, folks!), I'd get in bed, feel the weight of my cat on my feet, and wish I had someone I actually wanted to share a life with curling up behind me.

I want to fuck someone I actually like, maybe even love. I hate how difficult that is to find. Sometimes, these wants feel like a betrayal of all the hard work I've done to become myself, like I'm abandoning my strong, self-reliant core. After all, loneliness is too close to neediness, and everybody knows there are few things worse than a needy woman. I can say, "I want some dick," and everyone will laugh their own *been there, done that* laugh. When I share that sentiment online, I might even get a few texts or DMs. Yet as soon as I say, "I want to be loved genuinely and tenderly," the silence thrown back at me is an echoing mockery.

Their pity calls to mind that ridiculous question, *Can women have it all*? Am I not allowed to have a man if I have a successful career? People manage jobs, relationships, children, and so much more all the time. I want to share the highs and lows of my professional life with someone; I want to be heard, supported, and encouraged as needed. In what world is that asking for too much? And how does wanting someone on my team mean I'm no longer my own person?

I know how to take care of myself, but I don't need to be alone forever. If the heavens open tomorrow and my perfect man falls into my lap (hey, Hozier, honey), I wouldn't attach myself to him like a leech and void my brain of any thoughts of my own. Nor would I need him to help me bathe, but it would certainly be more fun. Having a partner doesn't mean I would become an oppressed, helpless damsel succumbing to the patriarchy because I can't survive on my own. It would simply mean that I found someone I can have a drink with, who orders me a whiskey neat on the first date without thinking it's a proposal. Maybe even someone worthy of sharing my life.

And so, I'm working on letting go of the strange shame I feel for admitting that I—bold, independent feminist—want a good man as a partner. When I confess this feeling to my girlfriends, I have to force myself not to whisper, but they encourage me, tell me to write down my wants, to speak them out loud, to light candles.

I know there is no magic key. I can take care of myself, and I'm proud of that. I've learned and unlearned myself; I've broken the cycle of falling for emotionally abusive men who preyed on my fear of loneliness. It's okay to be alone. I just no longer want to be.

I will always be my mother's child: yes, a man is nice, but I am even nicer. I will write down my desires and speak them out loud. I will light my candles. And I will wait for the love I know I deserve.

Are You Having Sex?
Natalie Lima

You knew it in your bones: you were pregnant.

The first time you saw a gynecologist, you were seventeen. It was springtime in Miami, not yet so hot that you wished you lived elsewhere. A few days before, you stood nervously in your kitchen as you watched your mom warm up yesterday's black beans and rice. You interrupted her, finally, and told her that your vagina felt "off," a sensation you didn't recognize. Looking down at your groin, you let out an anxious laugh.

You weren't exactly sure why you were shy talking to her about this. Your mom had a vagina, too. She often shared the complications of having one—most important, how men would always want to touch it, so you needed to be careful. Ever since you could remember, she repeated this wisdom to you. It's why, before you attended slumber parties growing up, she'd stop you at the door and give long speeches about the places on your body that needed protecting.

"It's probably a yeast infection," she said. "But you're old enough that it would be good to go to the gynecologist anyway."

Your mom made an appointment at the local low-cost clinic with sliding-scale billing. A single mother, she made about fifteen dollars an hour managing housekeeping at a hotel with a giant golf course in a fancy suburb called Doral. But she always got you to the doctor if you needed it.

In the waiting room, you rifled through gossip magazines together. After an hour of worry building in your head—fear of your first vaginal exam—a nurse opened a door and called your name.

Your mom stood up, ready to accompany you, but you said, "No. Stay, please."

She nearly ignored you. But after taking a second look at your face, at the pleading in your eyes, she sat back down.

The nurse led you down a hallway that smelled like it had recently been mopped with dirty water. In the exam room, she told you to take off your pants and cover yourself with the thin sheet she handed over.

The doctor was a tall white lady in her forties. Her energy was strong and unsettling, nothing like the warmth of your favorite characters on *ER*. There were no hellos or pleasantries. No words of comfort offered for a first visit. Not even a smile.

After she asked you to relax and spread your legs wide, she sneered. "You know you don't have to shave to come to the gynecologist."

You felt the thick condescension in her tone and realized then that she assumed you knew nothing about your own anatomy, that you'd shaved because of your ignorance. You didn't respond to the comment, just nodded silently.

What were you supposed to say?

Within a year, you'd be admitted to every college you applied to: Northwestern, Bryn Mawr, Sarah Lawrence, and the University of Miami. Most would offer a full-ride scholarship. You'd be invited to fly out to each campus to help with your decision, sharing decadent meals with girls who grew up knowing how to pronounce *tartare*. Against the odds, in less than a year, you'd be the first in your family to finish high school.

Still, despite all the achievements, similar occurrences would happen throughout your life: white doctors second-guessing you, making you procrastinate and dread every necessary appointment, avoid important care.

The reason isn't singular, the possibilities many: your racial ambiguity, a Latinx last name, the neighborhood you came from, your fat body, your gender. The list could go on forever. That first visit to the gyno simply showed you what had always been there.

Your examination over, you walked back to the waiting room with a diagnosis of bacterial vaginosis. You handed your mother the script for two drugs: an antibiotic to clear up the BV and another for birth control.

"Are you having sex?" she asked, her voice sharp.

You tried to come up with something to say; your mom was scary when she was angry. She hit things, threw things, broke things. Years later, she'd go to therapy and deal with this fury, but at the time she could be unpredictable.

"I told the doctor about my heavy periods," you said. "She said it would help."

This was partially true. For a week each month, it was red like

Russia down there. The doctor mentioned lighter periods as an added benefit.

More fiercely, your mother asked: "So you're not having sex, then?"

You finally lied, shaking your head. When you went to the counter, your mom told the pharmacist not to fill the birth control.

That summer, the South Florida humidity was so thick it felt like it could drown you. In June, you met a beautiful older man named John. He was twenty-four, a boxer with golden skin that gleamed in the heat.

He'd approached you in a Puerto Rican restaurant while you ate chicken pasteles and pulled you into conversation. When he asked for your number, you noticed that his flip-phone screensaver was a shirtless photo of himself. Though you found it ridiculous and almost laughed, you punched in your number and saved it.

"I like to hit it raw."

This is how the guys said it in high school. They swaggered around the halls, trying to out-man each other by bragging about all the pussy that came flying their way, all the bitches they'd raw-dogged.

These were the same dudes who'd bad-mouthed the pregnant girl in your class. How she got knocked up because she let some fool *hit it raw*.

So as you came of age, you assumed that other teenage girls

allowed it, too. That it was almost a duty to make sure the guy you were having sex with derived as much pleasure as possible from it.

Eventually, you learned: if you don't let him hit it raw, you lose.

And if you let him hit it raw, you lose, too.

When John called to invite you to a small get-together at a local Ramada, you agreed. You felt safe because he told you to bring friends and assured you that his female cousin would also be there.

At the hotel, you all listened to reggaeton and drank cold Heinekens, until everyone left you and John alone in the room. The kissing started, of course, then the touching, and just as you pulled a condom from your purse, John stopped you, waving his hand with a request: "Could you let me stick it in for just a second? Two seconds tops?"

And though you'd never had unprotected sex, and though you said aloud, "We should use the condom," you finally agreed to just a moment of what he wanted.

He finished inside of you almost instantly. Before you could even say, *That's enough now.*

A month later, you were on the way to a free summer SAT prep class at the local university. As soon as the bus parked, you ran to the school's bathroom to vomit.

You knew it in your bones: you were pregnant.

In college, you read in a sociology journal that 50 percent of Latinas had a pregnancy by the age of twenty. You learned that about

51 percent of all pregnancies in the United States were unintended, disproportionately affecting women of color.

At the time, it bothered you that as smart as you felt, sitting in a dorm room at your elite university, you hadn't escaped that statistic.

As you've gotten older and read more on the matter, as it's become more openly discussed in mainstream outlets that cover sexual health, you've learned of the many circumstances that create this racial disparity. Poverty. Private versus public health insurance. Lack of sexual education. Lack of access to birth control. Lack of, lack of, lack of . . .

Your abortion didn't involve any protesters, which you'd tried to prepare for emotionally. No blood-covered signs, no shouting. Years later, you're still grateful for this. John dropped you off at the curb outside the clinic and handed you the money to pay for the procedure.

There were other women who, like you, sat in hospital gowns in the waiting room. Women of all different races and ages. As you looked them over, you wondered if they'd, too, been with a man who'd insisted on hitting it raw *for just a second.*

Halfway through undergrad, a friend of yours got pregnant. She was white, from a liberal, upper-middle-class home in Northern California. She was one of those girls you were secretly envious of because both her parents lived at home, had master's degrees, and regularly traveled around the world. They'd been to Antarctica. You didn't even know people could go to Antarctica.

One day, she told you about her abortion. She said it so nonchalantly, like she'd gone in for a simple teeth cleaning, that you almost thought she was kidding. When she revealed to her mom that she was pregnant, her mom didn't make a big deal, simply called the family gynecologist and set up an appointment for the same week. That was that.

You didn't tell her about yours, but you found yourself feeling jealous. For her, there was no clinic. No fear of protesters. No stress about how to pay for it.

Still, your envy felt misplaced. Her experience wasn't typical, but it was certainly ideal: the support she received and the convenience of the procedure. Because of her financial and cultural circumstances, your friend experienced a scenario that would've been impossible if she'd been poor, or couldn't take off work, or if she came from a religious family, or a conservative one. The list is long.

You don't blame your mother for the far-reaching outcomes of that first gynecological visit. Having grown up in foster care, she hadn't had a real mother of her own. Now that you're only a few years shy of the age she was when she was raising a teenage daughter, you know her reaction came from fear. She couldn't have wanted you in her situation: in her late thirties, two teenagers in tow, the mediocre man who'd impregnated her missing in action.

What should a society expect of people who start in the margins? Women are made to traverse this world, dodging dicks left and right. We're hunted, taught to avoid rape in infinite ways: don't dress too sexy, don't smile too much, don't drink too much, don't walk home alone too late at night. And to top it all off, when the inevitable moment arrives, when a man wants to have sex and a woman doesn't, she must be polite when she declines.

After your abortion, you hid the paperwork for the procedure, all the directions for aftercare. You took the warnings about severe cramping and the potential for heavy bleeding and tucked them into a notebook inside a dresser.

You didn't say a word about it to your mother. You came home and spent the afternoon lying on the couch, watching television, waiting for the cramps to pass.

Six months later, well into your senior year, your mother discovered the paperwork while searching for something else. She called out your name, and when you saw her face, her eyes glued to the medical forms, you steeled yourself for the fury. All you can remember now is the screaming, the repetition of *I knew you were having sex. You liar. I knew.*

She picked up a glass and threw it at the wall, shards dancing over the tile floor.

The two of you never spoke of it again.

A fact: having access to birth control by age twenty reduces a woman's chances of living in poverty.

Your mom gave birth to you at twenty. You wonder if she'd ever had access to birth control.

When you talk to girlfriends now about sex with men, about how often cis male partners find ways to avoid using condoms, the societal expectation is clear: the onus to use protection is completely and consistently on the partner with a uterus.

You mull this over while helping high school seniors prepare their college applications, girls who are the same age you were when you had sex for the first time. Each one has a dream, and each a special gift. There's the natural-born leader, the killer storyteller, the problem-solver, the math whiz. You were just like them at seventeen, wanting to create a life with the talents you'd been given, knowing there'd be obstacles, judgments passed on your choices.

The stakes are even higher for young women today. With conservatives' antiabortion long game beginning to bear fruit—first in Texas, banning procedures after six weeks, and other states eagerly following suit—the war on women's bodies continues. The fact remains that when abortion is outlawed, abortions don't stop. *Safe* abortions do.

You hope these girls know more about their bodily autonomy than you did as a teenager. You hope they aren't afraid to speak up at the gynecologist. To speak up to their mothers. To speak up if they overhear boys bragging about hitting it raw. To push back. You hope these girls, as they become women, know what you didn't: that they can ask for more.

Queers Respecting Queers
Kristen Arnett

Current queer culture allows us to move forward with
fresh ideas about what bodily autonomy means, yet there
are those who still cling to the tropes of lesbians past.

I'm in a packed karaoke bar waiting for the bathroom. The music
is loud. Someone's singing Miley Cyrus—poorly. My friends are
sitting at a nearby table, poring over plastic binders full of songs
to choose their next ones.

A woman in line bumps into me. Repeatedly. She's waving
around her overly full drink. It spills. Some of it drips down her
hand, some lands on my shirt. Splashes daub the concrete floor
between us. She's much shorter than me and leans in close to say
something with a drunken grin. More of her cocktail drips from
her half empty glass. She reaches for my arm. At first, I assume
she's apologizing. But when she leans in closer and yells that she
thinks I'm hot, I realize she's drunker than I'd thought. And now
she's grabbing my arm more forcefully. And she's trying to wrap
her arm around my waist. I lean away, nearly overturning her in my
haste to extricate myself, but she's still trying to put her lips on me:
my ear, maybe, to talk, or possibly my mouth. I leave the line I've
been waiting in for over ten minutes and hope I don't piss myself.

Does the woman find someone else to lean on and make out with? Maybe. That's beside the point. The issue itself becomes a question, which begets more questions, ones I've asked myself a thousand times since coming out: What am I willing to put up with just so I can be at a gay bar? What boundaries will I let women cross? Do safe queer spaces actually exist?

When I was young and closeted, watching the world happen one way and feeling another way internally, I had to pretend. Like many others in this situation, I emulated the straight people around me. I put up posters of boys because all my friends did; I talked about which guys from class I found attractive, though I was secretly crushing on the girls; I went to movies and collectively swooned over male celebrities I had no interest in. I grew up in an extremely conservative Southern Baptist home. I didn't know any gay people; or if I did, they certainly weren't out to me.

I learned how to pass, developed an understanding of how I needed to behave in order to Not Be Seen. To make my readily apparent queerness, simmering just below the surface, as undetectable as humanly possible.

While closeted, I was also overly judicious about consent—so afraid that my cover might be blown, and so uninterested in dating men or even thinking about them sexually, that I was well aware of boundaries and how I needed to move through the world. I averted my eyes whenever I changed clothes in a locker room or in a bedroom crowded with friends at a sleepover. If I didn't look at anyone's naked body, then I wasn't doing anything wrong.

So when I came out in my twenties, I had to relearn how to interact with my peers. It was like puberty all over again: struggling with how to talk to women I was interested in, or even just to other queer friends. What did queer people bond over? Movies, books, television? Did their interests always have to be queer? I found myself navigating the uncharted waters of a delayed adolescence.

How does a person learn to socialize as a lesbian when they don't know any other lesbians? Or when they don't see themselves represented in media? We look to the places where we do see ourselves. On the internet, for starters. I pored over web pages and how-to guides. About lesbian sex, sure, but also about how to interact with other women. I learned the stable of jokes that pepper lesbian culture: the idea of U-Hauling, or the one about the turkey baster. How we've all dated each other's exes. How we all have sex with our friends.

I had so many questions about my queerness. And so I tried to frequent gay spaces, even though I felt that every other lesbian already knew everything and I was left behind, struggling to catch up.

Years later, I know this sentiment wasn't grounded in truth. There's no timeline, no true measurement of queerness. But in the moment, the situation felt dire.

A show like *The L Word*, with its bevy of gorgeous lesbians, was something I clung to as I tried to figure out who the hell I actually was. Episodes were crammed full of sexual liaisons and trysts, something I'd been desperate to see—the nearest comparison was porn, which was obviously engineered with the heterosexual male in mind and didn't care to unpack queer intimacy—but there was also so much drama. Friends sleeping with friends. Coworkers sleeping together. Strangers meeting and hooking up at clubs.

Exes getting back together only to lie to each other and break up again. And so many people cheating on each other. With women they knew and women they didn't.

I knew this wasn't logical—real-life relationships didn't function like this, not in any way I was familiar with—but when I went online or talked to the handful of queer women I met in my night-school classes, I'd hear the inevitable phrases: "She's such a Shane" or "They're so in love, like Bette and Tina."

Boundaries in these fictional relationships were crossed and toxic, and they quickly became signifiers of how I thought all lesbian relationships functioned.

Sometimes it's hard to unpack what we mean by a safe space. Safe from what, exactly?

As a fellow at an LGBTQIA writing retreat I attended—one that continues to be life-affirming, from long-lasting friendships to guidance and mentorship from seasoned authors—I found safety in being around those who wouldn't judge me based solely on my sexuality. It felt good to be around other people who identified as queer, with no expectation that I should explain my life and my choices. I also thought it meant that when we drank—and we drank a lot—I didn't need to worry about men touching my body without my consent. I'd been out for years by that time; I was in a long-term relationship with another woman. I felt secure in my boundaries and expectations.

One evening, a woman I'd been friendly with for most of the week suddenly came up behind me and stuck her hands into the front pockets of my jeans. Everyone in the room laughed, including me. I pulled her hands out—I was singing along to Bon Jovi into a wine bottle microphone—but she jammed them right back in. More laughter from everyone. The woman stumbled after me, grabbing for my ass. I kept moving, turning in circles, trying to ward her off.

"Oh, let her," someone called out. "She's just a baby gay. She doesn't know any better."

I let the woman chase me around the room a little more, until eventually another writer took pity on me and escorted her out so she could puke and sleep it off.

I went to bed feeling weird, and I woke up feeling even worse. I realized the whole situation had reminded me what it felt like to be at a bar and have an unwanted man try to talk, to push, taking my *no* as merely a starting point on the way to *yes*.

I began discussing this phenomenon with close friends in the queer community. These were conversations had in private, over drinks in our homes or at a low-key bar. It felt safer to voice my questions to people I knew intimately, to ask people I trusted, "What does it mean that queer people sometimes disregard boundaries or consent?"

But I found it difficult to take this conversation online. After a woman replied to one of my tweets with an inappropriate comment about wanting to be tied up and spanked, I tweeted that regardless of orientation, it's inappropriate to send sexual comments to people who haven't expressly asked for them.

The immediate feedback I received was disheartening. More than one person asked why I was calling out queer people when we should really be focusing on the harmful behavior of men. My response—that no one should violate boundaries, regardless of gender—was met with resistance.

I wasn't sure there were any straightforward answers, and I'm still not. I can only speak to my own experience as a white cis lesbian. Still, so much of my understanding has relied upon engaging with my queer community. My questions were confusing and difficult to parse alone: Should I call out women for this behavior when men so often get away with it? What is the cost of my callout? Of my silence?

I had a friend from undergrad who identified as straight for most of her life and later came out as queer. And when she started drinking at parties after coming out, she'd make a lot of comments to women—including me—about our bodies, how sexy we were, how she wanted to kiss us. She discussed the kind of sex she'd want to have if she wasn't married. At one party, she tried lifting the shirt of another close friend.

It became a running joke: that she liked to get "handsy" with people when she got drunk, that she groped her friends.

No one called it groping, though. Instead, we called it "loosening the libido." We joked about the fact that young queers (not young in age, necessarily, but in time out of the closet) didn't understand that the rules of consent applied to everyone. Boundaries were boundaries. But no one talked about that. We laughed instead. We shrugged it off.

After my marriage ended, I went back on dating apps and started frequenting queer bars. It was surreal to inhabit these places again, to navigate them as a person who better understood who I was and what I was looking for in partners. It also meant figuring out other people's boundaries.

At the time, I wasn't ready to date seriously and was looking for purely one-night stands or casual evenings out at a bar. I clearly conveyed this to everyone I met on the apps. Often, women would tell me this was fine, but when we'd meet up for drinks, things would pivot. They would try to pressure me, say they knew what I really wanted, that it wasn't fulfilling to only hook up. On one occasion, I showed up to find a woman significantly younger than she'd claimed to be, by at least ten years. When I confronted her about this, she laughed it off, claiming that she wanted to date women who were older than her, and if she didn't lie, she wouldn't get what she wanted. Plus, most of the women she lied to ended up changing their minds about dating her, she said. She'd been able to convince them.

Eventually, I began to avoid gay bars altogether. It had become literally and physically difficult to disentangle from people, especially when there was crying or yelling involved.

If I'd already articulated what I wanted and what I didn't, shouldn't those clearly defined lines be respected? Wouldn't I expect the same standard of consent regardless of gender or sexual orientation? Our (sexist) cultural assumptions that women are less aggressive than men, that they're "safer" to be around, has meant a total lack of discussion about the problems that occur when boundaries are crossed. The transgression is either considered a random outlier—a moment of erratic behavior with no bearing on the larger group—or it's simply glossed over: because it's coming from a queer woman, it's an inherently safe, nonthreatening act.

Too often, women told me they assumed I was joking when I said I wasn't interested.

I'll ask again: What do I mean when I say *safe*? What do I mean when I say *queer*? What do I mean about any of it?

The truth is, I don't know what I want from future spaces.

I do know that I want my body to be its own valuable, safe commodity, for myself alone. I want people to respect it, and by that I mean I want people to treat it the way I would like it to be treated; for everyone to understand that my body is mine and their body is theirs, and that all bodies need to be respected. I struggle with the fact that current queer culture allows us to move forward with fresh ideas about what bodily autonomy means, yet there are those who still cling to the tropes of lesbians past: the U-Hauls, the turkey basters, the cheap jokes. These tropes limit our ability to have crucial talks about queer consent. They're not just jokes; they're conversation enders.

It's true that I didn't address my discomfort with the leaning, spilling woman at the queer karaoke bar. Instead, I went back to my friends and took a few gulps of my beer. Now, I wonder about times that I may have made other people uncomfortable. Maybe I said something inappropriate, touched someone's arm, tried to dance too close to a stranger.

Boundaries—erected, meant to keep out or to hold close and contain—are significant in that they often lack nuance. And I don't mean just physically. The way that I use writing to understand my place in queer spaces means that certain words are invitations, but other words are barriers. I am working to explain myself and my own personal experience, but I am also attempting to explain the behavior of others. Language itself has boundaries. It allows us to convey ideas and express ourselves. I can only speak for myself.

But at the same time, language cannot include everything. It inevitably excludes ideas and thoughts, entire groups of people. We wield it shakily at times. We struggle to connect. We fail. Language simultaneously limits and empowers. I want to think there are better ways to understand each other, better ways to listen and to care. To accept the word *no*. To freely discuss the value of queer consent. To respect other queer bodies so we can continue to respect our own.

Big Second-Wife Energy
Minda Honey

I'd wanted a man who would let me love
him without restraint. I hadn't considered
how his love should feel in return.

Divorced Dad kissed me beside a car he thought was mine. It was January, but for that brief moment, I didn't feel the cold. A light snow shook down over everything. I was wearing earmuffs. We were a Hallmark card.

I wanted to bury my hands in the pockets of his peacoat, pull him toward me, and kiss some more. Instead, I smiled, said good night, and walked toward my actual car. When I got home, I opened a fresh notebook and wrote a love letter to commemorate our first date. One of many, I felt certain.

The previous spring into summer, I'd dated a too-attractive man, a recent arrival to my city. I'd felt chosen. The compliments. The dinners. That thing with his tongue. My heart turned toward him, and he turned away. Days between texts. Lies about other women. He was one of those men who wants your attention but not your love. I tried not to care, but I was tired of those men. By the end of July, neither his height nor his hotness nor the absolute way he worshipped my body was enough to keep me.

Summer into fall, I took up long-distance with a man who'd been in my orbit for years. I desperately wanted him to be the last person I ever dated. I wanted to love this man. To never again be reeled in and cast out like I had been that summer. I was emotionally transparent with him. I used my words. Ultimately, we parted ways but remained friends, and I appreciated the growth in myself that had made that possible.

And now, I was hopeful I'd met someone who shared my newfound emotional maturity. That this was a man who could stand in the light of my love without needing to shield himself from its brightness.

I met Divorced Dad on New Year's Eve, a few days before my birthday. My friends insisted thirty-five was a milestone year. To me, it felt like a nothing-special age, like twenty-two or thirty-one. But they were right, because apparently your midthirties are when all the men who married without hesitation in their twenties return to the dating pool like children coming out of hiding at the end of hide-and-go-seek—*olly olly oxen free!* And here was my first divorcé.

Divorced Dad recognized me from around town, and I was friends with his business partner, but somehow he and I had never met before this party. He was drunk. I was sober. He was controlling the music and insisted on playing the new Danny Brown for me ("He's not doing that weird voice anymore"). He swayed by my side the entire night, though when my crew announced we were leaving, he didn't ask for my number. I decided to get his Instagram handle instead. Low stakes, I thought.

"Don't worry about the woman in all the photos," he said. "I'm newly divorced."

I wasn't surprised that he'd been married. While I was moving around the country letting fuckboys crash into my emotions like sledgehammers, everyone in my small southern hometown had coupled up, and I'd returned home to find few options for a suitable partner. As happy as I was with my life, it was hard to be back in my city and not focus on what I didn't have. Why was I the only one without a match?

I, too, wanted to participate in the coupledom central to this stage of life. I wanted a man who'd be my date-night default. Someone who'd plan my surprise birthday party, who Girls' Night would be an excuse to get away from, but who I'd always be relieved to return home to. Someone whose income combined with mine would make buying a home possible. Someone who, when he looked into the future, could make out the faint outline of us.

Maybe my someone had been another woman's marriage mishap. Maybe I was meant to be a second wife, the wife you choose after discovering who you really are. Maybe a man who'd been married once before was more likely to do it again. I was willing to be the second, as long as it also meant being the last.

In Divorced Dad's Instagram feed, I found casual shots of him and his first wife grinning at each other over matching pint glasses at a trendy beer garden. Their church wedding. Their curly-haired child. Their overseas travels. The most recent photo cropped tight around their smiling faces. Simultaneous evidence that love doesn't always last, but the decisions you make in love often do.

When Divorced Dad said it, we were in his car cruising toward what was probably the only restaurant where he could get a Valentine's Day reservation on such short notice.

I wasn't expecting him to say he loved me. We'd been dating for less than two months, and just a few days ago, over tea in my living room, when my mentee had asked Divorced Dad and me about our plans for the fourteenth, I'd said that I didn't know what *he* was doing because *we* didn't have any plans.

When my mentee left, Divorced Dad looked at me sheepishly and said he was supposed to play video games at his best friend's house Friday night, and besides, we hadn't been dating long enough to celebrate, right?

At my bedside in the next room was the notebook of love letters I'd been writing him after every date. I'd planned on gifting him the collection in a box with a hand-tied bow.

"How long do we have to wait before it's okay to celebrate our happiness?" I asked.

He made the dinner reservation.

When he confessed that he was getting me the most obvious gift for Valentine's Day, I looked at the small bouquets arranged around my house and asked, "Flowers?"

He just laughed.

The next day, a knock came at my door. It was a girl from the coffee shop across from his office and next door to my favorite florist, it should be said—holding an oversized chocolate chip cookie (which I do not like) and the coffee shop's premade love-song playlist (full of music I do not listen to). I tried not to feel hurt. We hadn't been dating very long; maybe he didn't know me well enough to pick out a suitable gift.

Which is what made the "I love you" completely unexpected.

He glanced at me for my reaction, his car veering slightly

toward the semi passing us on the left. I maintained my neutral expression while I thought about what to say. My silence gone on too long, he panicked.

"Why did I say that? I've messed up everything!" he said.

I assured him it was fine. How he felt was how he felt; I just wasn't there yet.

At the same time, I didn't want his emotional openness to collapse in on itself. *This is a man I can love*, I thought. *Eventually.*

I held the box of love letters in my lap and played with the tails of the bow. Earlier that week, he'd called me mid–anxiety attack, telling me that his ex had just served him with divorce papers. I was surprised: the night we met, he'd told me he was already divorced. But there was no time for me to process this news, his need to be consoled too immediate.

And now it was Valentine's Day and he'd said he loved me. It's not quite the right holiday to say, "I don't love you," and then, "Did you lie to me about being divorced?"

So, I held in both.

I began to feel a little foolish about the love letters. How I'd used a different-colored pen for each one, and my best cursive. Swooping, looping, linked letters. Maybe I was being childish and adult love was about two names on a mortgage and less about dinner on Valentine's Day. Maybe divorced dads operated differently, moved at a faster pace, and were less sentimental about relationship milestones. He owned his own home and kept it tidy. He ran a business. He met with multiple lawyers, weekly, over divorce matters. I was certain the failed marriage and fatherhood had made him a grown-up. Now, it was my turn to grow up, too, to shift my perspective on what adult relationships looked like.

I told myself I needed to skip the fantasy and get straight to the practical.

Divorced Dad told me his child was coming to stay for the summer, but that I wouldn't be meeting him. No part of me wants children, so I assured him the kid didn't have to meet "daddy's special friend" until his high school graduation, if that's what Divorced Dad wanted.

But as the weeks passed, he changed his mind. I didn't.

I wasn't ready to even lightly role-play stepmotherhood, to pose in Perfect Family Moments with some other woman's child. I worried meeting his child so early in our relationship might move me closer to his ex-wife and their past life together, making me a secondary character in *their* marriage plot, rather than a lead in my own love story.

My parents divorced when I was twelve, and my heart never recovered. On a Minda-themed episode of *Family Feud*, if the contestants were asked to name my worst fears, divorce would ding out near the top of the list.

The thing about dating Divorced Dad was that it was difficult for me not to see my own father in him. This wasn't new for me; I regularly caught glimpses of my father in the men I dated.

Sometimes I found myself feeling more compassionate for my father and what it must've been like for him to live a life divided between his family, his work, and what he actually wanted. Other times, I just felt triggered. Like when Divorced Dad showed up late for a dinner I'd spent hours making. I could smell beer on his breath as he claimed that a meeting with his business partner—who didn't drink—had run late.

I didn't ask any questions. I just stood there, a foot shorter than him, wiping my hands on my apron, feeling like my mother.

Divorced Dad wanted me to believe it was okay I hadn't said "I love you" in return, but when we had sex and I was about to hit that crescendo, he'd press his whole mouth to my ear and snarl his truth, hot and wet: *You* will *love me, too.*

He didn't like to talk about the divorce but often did anyway; it was a major thing happening in his life. Curled up on his couch or mine, he'd relay something he'd texted his ex or how she'd sniped at him over the phone, what his lawyers wanted to do or how he was attempting to work the system in his favor.

It's difficult to fall in love with someone as they're falling out of love with someone else. New relationships require a certain naïveté about what a person is capable of doing to those closest to them, but divorce makes the worst of a partner immediately visible. I struggled not to sympathize with this other woman. Each act of assholery toward the mother of his child became a point on the spectrum of what was possible in our own relationship.

I kept wondering: how would I feel if I was the woman I'd seen on Divorced Dad's Instagram, who he drunkenly told some new love interest not to worry about?

In March, Divorced Dad came over to make me dinner, then kept me company while I stress-packed for a conference. I assumed he was over to help calm my nerves about my trip, but as I listened to SZA and worked my way through my mental checklist, he lay on my bed and began playing Sonic the Hedgehog on his phone. With the sound on.

Annoyed, I asked him to put his phone on silent.

"It's not as much fun with the sound off," he pouted.

I pointed out that I was already listening to music.

He said, "Fine. I'll just leave the sound effects on."

I stared at him, Sonic collecting gold rings the soundtrack to my disbelief. Softly I said, "You are making it very difficult for me to spend time with you."

The phone went quiet.

A few weeks after I returned from the conference, after another round of passive-aggressive I-love-you sex, Divorced Dad and I met up for a walk on one of those evenings when spring has almost fully slipped into summer. A block from my house, he asked if I wanted to get a pizza that weekend.

I stopped walking. "Actually, I want to break up," I said.

Standing there on the sidewalk in the fading sunshine, he seemed stunned. "But I had big plans for us," he said.

I'd wanted a man who would let me love him without restraint. I hadn't considered how his love should feel in return. That he might whisper aggressions in my ear as if they were sweet nothings. That even while dating the kind of grown-up required of perma-coupledom, I might still feel the same kind of alone I'd felt when I was single.

Later, in bed by myself, without the sound of Sonic's rings crashing in the background, I thought, *Wow, I really do want to die alone.*

But for the first time in all my years of picking on myself, my mind responded with kindness: *As long as I die happy, who cares?*

I was thirty-five years old when I realized happiness and being single aren't mutually exclusive. If a man is the worst part of my life, the remedy is an easy one: dump him.

Keeping Divorced Dad around didn't mean my life became any more put together, and my life after we broke up didn't devolve into an embarrassing mess. My life was fine. *I* was fine.

I thought that dating men who had a veneer of responsible, capable adulthood signaled to the outside world that I knew my Mr. Rights from my Mr. Wrongs, that I could make good choices, but those men proved to be just as unfulfilling and emotionally damaging as the dude who does that one thing with his tongue but can't text back in a timely manner.

I was mistaken in thinking the men I date are a barometer for how well I'm adulting. In this small city that I love living in but where I struggle to find love, my options seem to be to stay single and zen or date the people who are available to me. Sometimes, at the expense of my heart, I choose chaos.

This kind of dating in my thirties feels like I'm moving the sliding weights on an old-fashioned scale: I'm striving for that careful balance between staving off loneliness in the short term and protecting my happiness in the long term. But what I really want is to step off the scale for good, into a relationship that's more than a simulacrum of all the things I need from love.

By June, two more divorced dads expressed their interest in me, but only one made it from my phone into my bed. With his mouth pressed against my ear, the only thing I heard, hot and wet, was, *Do you like that?*

A Father's Day miracle.

Loved Out Loud
Keah Brown

For the first time in my life, I'm happy being single.

The two situationships I found myself in at the age of twenty-eight happened a handful of months after I came out as bisexual. I'd honestly never thought I would. The fear of being too late for love or too old to be queer after a fruitless year on dating apps—or, worst of all, losing my family—kept me in the closet. But I was tired of hiding a truth I'd known since I was like ten, watching *Gotta Kick It Up* and quietly swooning over the character of Daisy as she swooned over her boyfriend, who was also super cute.

I came out to Twitter first, the way you do—in a hotel in California on the last night of a work trip, watching *Stepmom* and eating Shake Shack. Twitter was immediately supportive and encouraging. My queer and straight best friends expressed their pride in me for living my truth out loud before cracking jokes about how they already knew. I sat for a few moments in that bubble of joy and freedom.

But then my twin sister was immediately alerted by one of her friends who followed me. Later, this friend reassured me that it was not with malicious intent. Still, my hand was shaking as I replied to my sister's text that simply asked if "I was gay." I told her I was bisexual and went to bed.

At the airport the following morning, I came out to the rest of the family in our group chat before fear got the best of me again. I put my phone on airplane mode and landed back East to a lot of questions and some lighthearted jokes. The first few days of being out were weird and rough for a variety of reasons. However, instead of disowning me, like TV shows and films had led me to believe would happen, my family continued to embrace me. I'm one of the lucky ones in that regard. I wouldn't say they understand me completely or that we don't have hard days, but they love me and want me to be happy, and that's enough.

I've walked through life as a Black, queer, disabled woman for twenty-nine years. I have cerebral palsy that impacts the right side of my body, so I walk with a limp; the fingers on my right hand bend and remain that way. I have a delayed reaction time and limited motor skills. There's nothing wrong with any of these things, that much I know now, but many other people don't. In high school, every guy wanted me to put in a good word for him to a friend or my sister, but any compliments I heard directly and indirectly were in the vein of "Keah's kinda cute, but her hand," or "She's not ugly, but I'd never ask her out." I learned to laugh off these comments and pretend they didn't get to me—but of course, I often cried myself to sleep. I thought their words meant I was the ugliest of ogres, not even worthy of being loved in secret. I grew up in a city where everyone knows everyone, and the thing they all seemed to know was that they didn't want me.

My first situationship was with a nonbinary person I'll call Mia. They followed me on Twitter for a while, but I didn't really notice because of the number of followers I have. I know that sounds like a brag, but sometimes people get lost in the shuffle.

Mia and I exchanged flirty tweets before I messaged them privately, and so it began. It was fun and exciting—remember, I'd never been desired out loud before. Rejection and setting up my friends was what I knew; that's who I was and who I thought I would always be.

With Mia, things were different. We talked about family, career dreams, meeting up postpandemic, and about how much we wanted each other.

But before long something shifted, and we started arguing. I often felt like I was on pins and needles, hoping they wouldn't be angry about a word I used or something innocuous I liked (examples ranged from my Paramore fandom to celebrity crushes). I was afraid that if I didn't apologize for these little nothings, I would lose out on my chance at love—which led me to accept the kind of treatment that I would have seen as a red flag if it had happened to a friend or family member. But the flags were never red enough to me, a person who knew what loneliness felt like because I'd lived inside of it. Who would want to go back to that?

My memories of past rejection came rushing back. In high school, in that city where everyone knew everyone and none of them wanted me, I was naive enough to think something magical would happen to me anyway. Instead, I spent high school dateless and depressed, desperate for some boy who didn't matter to say he loved me under the harsh lights of our school hallways. Year after year I wished and waited for someone to love me—and therefore save me. I dreamed of a big prom ask that would rival the scenes in the romantic movies I loved so much.

If Mia didn't want me anymore, who would? I came out late, I didn't drive, and every time I entered a public place, some people saw fit to stare at me because of my limp.

My experience with Mia ended after a few more stops and starts, during a huge argument in which we traded insults, trying our best to hurt each other. We were definitely a wrong fit, so different that our initial attraction couldn't save us from the inevitable end.

Still, once it was finally and truly over, I worried that I'd missed my shot. After all, it had taken me twenty-eight years to have my first one; I didn't want to wait another twenty-eight for another. I spent a lot of time beating myself up for not sticking it out, even though I knew the situation wasn't healthy. This was something my therapist and I worked through during a lot of tear-filled sessions, slowly rebuilding the confidence and joy I'd lost.

I hate the phrase "You have to love yourself before someone else loves you." It makes love conditional, and I also don't think it's true. However, I was miserable when I was constantly tearing myself down under the guise of preparation for the so-called real world's reaction to me. Before I met either Mia or Ella, I began my journey of self-love. It's been a steady process with bumps and setbacks. I find that it's harder than people believe to get out of bed every day and choose to verbalize positive traits when you're used to hating every physical thing about yourself but the color of your skin. I do it every single day, though, because I know how exhausting it is to beat myself up before others get the chance.

So when Ella came into my life, I was feeling good, finally over

Mia and recognizing the importance of taking care of myself and trusting my gut. I'd worked tooth and nail to replace my negative self-talk with positive reinforcement. I began complimenting myself out loud, regardless of how silly it felt. In therapy, I continued the work of taking people at their word, so much so that when anyone complimented me, I said thank you instead of launching into a self-deprecating joke—and started to see qualities worth liking in myself, too. Something shifted.

Ella and I had been following each other on Twitter for a long time; I always thought she was cute, but I never tried to get at her. One random night, I tweeted about how I missed flirting but didn't want to get back on dating apps (we know what a hellscape *they* can be). She responded with a *Lilo and Stitch* GIF and I messaged her privately to say I liked the GIF before I signed off and went to bed.

In the morning, she responded, and so it began again.

Because of everything that had happened with Mia, I went in cautiously. I was scared to open up but also excited that I was getting another chance to explore a romantic connection and see where it took me. We had a lot in common, similar hopes and dreams and pop-culture affinities (minus her love of science fiction). I often pictured us together on a couch, me falling asleep with my head on her lap as she watched whatever it is they do in sci-fi.

I feel like I could've loved Ella if things had been different for us both. We knew that ending it was important when it began to feel like we were trauma bonding rather than building the foundation of a relationship. We agreed that we weren't ready for each other. Sometimes you meet people at the wrong time and can't be what they need, even if you want to be.

Despite the end of both situationships, there's something beautiful in the fact that my first two forays into romantic territory were queer relationships. As a woman who thought she would go to the grave in the closet, I think it's special to have had those first experiences with queer people.

Having only been out for three years, there's still a lot left for me to explore, and I hope to get that opportunity. For much of my life, I believed I'd take any willing man and stuff down every part of me that ever desired anyone other than men. But these nascent relationships, and seeing how my other queer friends navigate their prospective relationships, fill me with hope where jealousy and sadness once resided. I used to joke with my friends that I was a catch and I didn't understand why no one else understood that. Now, though, I feel like I might actually be a catch, and that there are many parts of me that make me worth pursuing—not only the things Mia and Ella saw value in, but more important, what I see value in: my humor, my loyalty, my wide and bright smile, my enthusiasm, my gentle nature.

The biggest differences between my endings with Mia and Ella is that with Ella, we ended amicably and maturely, with a respect and honesty I'm not sure I would've been able to muster had I not experienced the ending with Mia.

Ella showed me what I deserve in my future partner—man, woman, or gender-nonconforming person. She reinforced that I can have standards, that I should be with someone who shows up when I need them to and doesn't disappear after one disagreement.

From Mia, I learned to be more careful about who I let in. I'm not trying to be shady, but truly, the most important thing I took away from my first situationship was that I should never be condescended to, gaslighted, or shamed.

In both cases, I only realized much of what I wanted and deserved from them after the fact.

No one leaves any situationship with clean hands; I don't believe I was completely innocent in either. The first I entered into with fear, my own abandonment issues, and the inability to speak up for myself. With Ella, I carried over the fear and needed too much reassurance that I was desirable. We all come with baggage, and mine came with second-guessing luggage tags.

Nevertheless, these experiences changed something within me. I once believed the only person who would ever think I was truly worthy of romantic love was myself. But my friends, family, and even my therapist believe that more romantic situations—and maybe one day, actual relationships—will happen for me in the future. I don't have a crystal ball, but after having two almost-relationships, a third doesn't seem so impossible. Compared to where I was before coming out, I know that I'm much better off now, simply because I'm no longer waiting for the kind of inherent validation that comes with dating.

The reality is that I will likely be lax in ways I shouldn't be in future relationships, and that I will definitely mess up in some way, because I'm human. Still, I'm grateful for my new standards and that I've articulated my desires for my future.

A few weeks after my ending with Ella, I tweeted that I was happy being single. I didn't post it to try to hurt her—I often tweet things that come to mind, forgetting that people actually read them. The truth is, it was a genuine insight. For the first time in my life, I'm happy being single. I'm not opposed to meeting someone, but I'm not actively looking or sulking about my relationship status either.

When I was single in high school and college, it wasn't because I wanted to be but because I'd been taught that someone like me wasn't desirable. Now, my singlehood is a choice. I do hope that my soul mate is out there waiting for me. They're probably cuddled up with someone else thinking they're in love—it's cute. I'll see them soon. But for now, I'm happy to slide into a few more DMs, flirt with a few more people, live my life, and fall deeper in love with myself while I wait for them.

A New Kind of Heroine
Laura Bogart

Freed from the concerns about whether my body
was fuckable, I could make a tender peace with it.

I still have no idea what it looks like for a woman who can't physically be carried off into the sunset to find love, or at least the kind of passion that gives us a home in our own bodies. When I see lustful fat women on-screen, they're often clowns, like Melissa McCarthy's caricature of ungainliness in *Bridesmaids*—a woman who jokes about downing hoagies and climbing a series of increasingly disconcerted men "like trees"; whose grand moment of seduction entails slinging a foot, clad in a boxy sandal, to trap a man inside his airplane seat as she rubs her ample stomach and refers, quite winkingly, to the treasures of her "undercarriage." Her appetites for sex and food are so grotesque that they're comically extreme, even in a movie touted for its gross-out bawdiness. It takes me back to my school cafeteria, a rictus of faces laughing at me, and the first time I was ever punished for my desire.

Middle school is already a crucible for daydreamy kids, but even more so for a girl like me: fat and awkward, dimpled thighs, flabby arms, hips and belly that stubbornly resisted the baby-doll dresses and plaid skirt sets in vogue at the time. The hallways echoed with whispers when I simply passed by. Bus rides were hotboxes of rolled eyes and hostile stares—and, oh yes, the inevitable elephant noises whenever I was forced to sit next to someone.

Still, I filled my diary pages with vivid fantasies: the tall boy with the beautiful fingers whose locker was next to mine defending me against the bullies; the sandy-haired boy who sat in front of me in history class, whose broad shoulders enticed me far more than the pioneers' struggles, asking me to a movie; or the freckled boy who wrote for the literary journal wanting to talk poetry and drink milkshakes at the mall. My hope was a blue-winged moth hovering over a flame, so much more poignant for how hard it had to work to stay aloft.

Then, one day, the sandy-haired boy approached me at lunch. He asked in a deeply tender voice if I would go to homecoming with him. Of course I would go with him! Did he need my phone number? I could give him my phone number. But as I pulled a page from my notebook—my pulse thumping throughout my body—I saw him turn and give the thumbs-up to the table of boys behind him.

Their laughter. His laughter. It was all I could hear. The sound was a fist that snatched the blue-winged moth and flung it into the hard wall of reality. Nobody was asking the fat girl to homecoming. Fat girls weren't to be pined for or desired. Certainly not loved. We were objects of ridicule or figures to be ignored.

And so, by my late twenties, the Technicolor realm of my fantasies had turned to a wash of gray: Why humiliate myself by pursuing men who would never want me, when I could at least give myself the small dignity of accepting the ones who did? There was the man who kissed my forehead with such tenderness when I told him I was a virgin, but who mistook the urethra for the clitoris. There was the man who knew where to find the clitoris, who wanted to be "Facebook official" a week into dating—which really involved hanging out at his place and fooling around—only to dump me for an ex he would go on to marry. To other men, I became a collection of body parts: a belly to fondle, breasts to smother a face in, a rear end to press the breath out of a man's body (if being sat on was his sort of thing). Never expecting to be seen as whole. Never enjoying myself. Certainly not having the kind of sex that my thinner cohorts seemed to be enjoying, encounters that made them cooler, more righteous and empowered.

Life seemed to offer me a cold binary of choice: I could keep dating (or trying to date), or I could preserve my dignity in solitude. I tried to imagine a woman with my body being embraced by a lover, his hands on the soft folds of her back—nothing spectacular in the gesture. Simple admiration. Like anyone else in love. But then the image dissolved. Gone, because I couldn't hold on to it. Gone, because I'd never seen it—not in ads, not on TV, not in movies.

Fat women aren't cast as the pixieish heroines of a rom-com or the lithe beauties of a cop drama; we do not appear in ads for bridal gowns or lingerie. Fat women never get to have coupon-night-at-Olive-Garden love. Or stroll-through-the-topiary-garden-by-moonlight love. Or even good old-fashioned knock-supper-off-the-kitchen-table-because-we-have-to-have-each-other kind of love. Sometimes I found a momentary delight in chat rooms and bedrooms, but it was never carried into daylight. Instead, it was usually followed by hours on the phone nurturing yet another "guy friend" through an entanglement with a thin woman he would forever like more than me, at least in the ways that mattered most, and nights alone watching shows and films that depicted supposedly empowered women as ancient warriors and modern-day boss bitches, brilliant scientists and FBI agents, chic singletons and conflicted suburban moms whose happy endings always involved a love interest because they were always svelte enough to deserve one.

The spinning sphere of media offers candy-colored visions of singledom straight from the glossy pages of lady magazines, filled with headlines like "Busting That Bloat to Help You Boss Up and Nail That Dream Job," and "The Wonder Woman Workout (Because You Know You Want Those Amazon Abs!)." That's not to mention the advertisements for jade eggs that increase the vibrations of our orgasms and Strippercize classes to get us toned enough to take charge in the bedroom. There are dating apps that explicitly brand themselves as offering zipless fucks for the TikTok generation, ones that, for all their lip-service glorification of kink and transgression, still feature models with whittled bellies and hip bones that could cut glass. Women can thirst unabashedly in pop songs and gender-bent "dude comedies" and demand to be sexually satisfied in the pages of magazines and on prestige dramas, but only if they're conventionally hot enough to spark lust in a typical straight guy.

A fat woman who dares to lust is a rebel, but not the cool kind. She's a deviant who must suffer humiliation. Even a show like *American Horror Story*, which purports to champion outcasts, takes delight in sinking its fangs into the tender hearts of fat characters. More than one episode has brought me to tears, like when the lone fat witch in season 3's titular *Coven*, played by Gabourey Sidibe, confronts an advancing minotaur by telling him that she, too, knows what it's like to be seen as a monster, then slides her hand down her pants and touches herself, because she's been made monstrous by her desperation and only another monster could ever want her. My tears came again, hot and violent, during an arc on the fourth season of *Freak Show*, wherein the hunky Lobster Boy's bedding of the Fat Lady is the final rung of his descent into alcoholic hell. As he looks at her, his face crumples with revulsion; sobbing, he buries his head in her chest. So grateful for the affection—however little it has to do with her, however tinged it is with disgust—she strokes his back. I wept from anger, but mostly from recognition.

According to popular culture, it seems women like me—dirty little secrets, throwaway bedmates, fetishes your buddies would deride you about—aren't entitled to desires of our own. We live in the liminal cosmos of mockery and neglect.

So, as I entered my thirties, I wrapped myself in my own company. I spun a cocoon of hobbies and friends, one lined with a dedication to my writing career. I wrote and sold a novel; I published essays in dream outlets. Freed from the concerns about whether my body was fuckable, I could make a tender peace with it. I could feel gratitude for heavy, sturdy thighs that let me take my dog for walks; a back that, soft folds and all, still allowed me to spend hours bent over a garden bed. Even my stomach, my great bane, began to seem innocuous, simply a part of me, rather than something to be fetishized or reviled. Once I stopped dating, stopped wanting to feel "normal" by pursuing sex like my thinner friends did, I reached a kind of benevolent quietude, safe and nourished in my own company—even if I never saw emotionally healthy, contented, and loved fat women in media.

When friends asked what was new in my life, my answer was always a byline or a report on how my tomatoes and peppers were faring, never a new man whose various behaviors required meticulous dissection over coffee or cocktails. Even if they were disappointed by my lack of a juicy love life, no one ever offered to set me up—after all, they consumed the same media I did, had been told the same stories I had. The romantic heroines of holiday Hallmark films shop at Ann Taylor, not Lane Bryant. My perpetual singledom didn't surprise anybody—and that fact felt like not so much a slap in the face but a series of bruising pinches all along the tenderest parts of my body. Despite myself, I still wanted a world where everyone can imagine a fat girl being cherished and desired.

Recently, we've been served some droplets of cool water in the desert of representation: Lizzo arrived like a voluptuous, flute-playing Venus rising from her clamshell, crooning tales of romantic travails and sexual conquests, glorying in costumes as glamorous and revealing as those of any of her thinner cohorts. Back in my twenties, if I'd seen her posing nude on her album cover—unabashed and addressing the camera with a gaze both sultry and defiant—I might've believed that I didn't have to apologize for my body, that I could ask for what I wanted in bed and be acknowledged outside of the bedroom. There are bestselling books like *Dumplin'*, about a fat girl who enters a beauty contest and wins the heart of her handsome crush, that was adapted into a Netflix film. And, of course, Jennifer Weiner's *Good in Bed*, arguably the best-known tale of a plus-size singleton, was picked up for film adaptation—although Mindy Kaling, the heroine, is decidedly more petite than the novel's protagonist, who ends up inspiring and later penning a column called "Loving a Larger Woman."

Though I'm reluctant to leave the shelter of my cocoon to spread my wings and circle the heat of desire, lately I catch myself scrolling through social media, searching for images of fat women in happy relationships, fat women in pinup looks, fat women dishing about the good sex they're having. Rare as they are, these images make me wonder if it's possible to try dating again—not as a desperate woman flinging herself at any man who would do her the favor, but as a woman who fully inhabits her body and knows that if she can't find a lover who treats her well, she'll be perfectly fine on her own.

I've helped to heal myself, and I know that I'm not without desire. I still long to touch and be touched, to look up in a moment of passion and catch my partner's face in blissful exaltation because he adores me, all of me. I still want my body to sing with pleasure. I still crave the comfort of a hand in mine, the warmth of being claimed in the daylight.

Sex and the Single Frump
Briallen Hopper

I've never looked less glamorous,
and I've never felt more at peace.

"You need to look glamorous every minute," writes Helen Gurley Brown, in a siren song from beyond the grave. I'm sure wherever she is now, she's perfectly turned out: face spackled with Max Factor Pan-Cake makeup, wig sleek and glossy, Chanel suit tailored close to the bone, and hunger pangs ignored, even in the afterlife.

I first read *Sex and the Single Girl* in my teens, and even though my style aspirations were more Courtney Love than *Cosmo* girl, I was swept along by the book's campy verve. I couldn't help being fascinated by Brown's brisk, bossy tone and her brash attempts to initiate the reader into her version of self-made beauty with advice like, "If your fat little tummy should have been lopped off two years ago, lop it off." Her unapologetic ruthlessness reminded me of the gruesome Brothers Grimm version of *Cinderella*, in which the stepsisters literally cut off their heels and toes to fit into the magic glass slipper.

I read the book with a dash of irony—I was partly in it for the retro references to wine-for-breakfast diets and pink silk Capri pants—but I was also susceptible to its messaging. I was genuinely overwhelmed by how out of control my body felt and how harsh the world seemed. Brown's drastic recommendations seemed proportionate to the pressure I felt to be perfect, or at least passable. I liked to imagine a future in which I, like Brown, would face a sexist system armed with thinness, bright lipstick, and an impeccable outfit.

Now I'm her worst nightmare.

My work-from-home wardrobe consists of a bunch of shapeless flannel nightgowns that my boyfriend calls "billowcases." I don't distinguish between sleepwear and daywear, and my hair hasn't been cut in almost a year. My toenails are streaked with faint traces of ancient polish that I haven't bothered to remove. I can no longer fit into most of my clothes, and I recently found my long-lost Fitbit under the radiator, literally gathering dust. I've never looked less glamorous, and I've never felt more at peace.

This truce with my looks was hard-won. I'm forty-two and I've definitely served my time with mainstream beauty standards. My hippie mom banned Barbie dolls, but it didn't matter; I was anorexic by thirteen, which later almost caused me to be uninsurable because it counted as a preexisting condition. As a high schooler, I begged my parents for a breast reduction that I didn't need and we couldn't afford, and covered my arms with third-degree cigarette burns. In my twenties, I dated someone who told me he'd broken up with a previous girlfriend—an eating disorder survivor like me—because she'd gained weight. Instead of hearing "Red flag!" I heard "Stay thin!"

For years I read feminist critiques of beauty and diet culture and agreed with them in theory, but I couldn't quite bring myself to put them into practice. Instead, I dealt with my ongoing anxiety and depression by restricting my eating, compulsively clothes shopping, and climbing endless flights of stairs.

Something had to give. I was exhausted.

In my midthirties, heartbreak, stress, and diet fatigue finally convinced me to change my relationship to my body and to clothes. I stopped counting calories and grew several sizes, gaining a new heftiness that made me feel both liberated and invisible. Instead of the fitted vintage outfits I favored as a young adult, I started wearing voluminous dresses and orthopedic flip-flops—mom or grandma fashion with no children or grandchildren to show for it. I even embraced frump as a kind of feminist aesthetic. I discovered and loved Emma Copley Eisenberg's classic essay "Notes on Frump: A Style for the Rest of Us," and I wrote my own admiring essays on frump icons Shirley Jackson and Grace Metalious, who embodied the kind of rumpled, dumpy, fat-white-lady-writer vibe I was heading for. I knew I'd arrived when a catcaller yelled at me, "Damn, those shoes look comfortable!"

Then a cancer scare and colon surgery made me temporarily incontinent, and a few months in adult diapers sounded the death knell of any residual aspirations to glamour I'd been clinging to. I welcomed the end of an era, spiritually ready to embrace a life of messy topknots and infrequent makeup.

Reveling in dishevelment has been a happy ending of sorts, and I'm grateful for it. I'm glad I'm done losing sleep over my curves and scars, at least for now.

Then again, like most happy endings, it's not that simple.

Who gets to be a frump? And who wants to be one?

When I was a fashion-conscious grad student applying for academic jobs, I had a practice interview with a powerful professor in my program—a white woman with plain gray hair who always wore nondescript clothes and no makeup. Instead of offering me substantive feedback on my performance, she sent an email blast to all the job candidates telling us to avoid colorful nail polish. She said she found it so distracting that it was impossible for her to concentrate on what interviewees were saying.

My nails had been painted red.

On the surface, the antifashion professor doesn't seem to have much in common with Helen Gurley Brown; in fact, they appear to be at opposite ends of the glamour spectrum. But as I've reread *Sex and the Single Girl*, I've realized that the professor's pronouncement against stylish manicures is strikingly similar to Brown's aversion to curves and her repeated warnings about wearing too much jewelry and looking "too Ubangi."

What unites these advice-giving women across the decades is their whiteness and the way they wield it. Implicitly or explicitly, they both define acceptable ways to look against the looks associated with Black women and other women of color.

As sociologist Sabrina Strings documents in her book *Fearing the Black Body: The Racial Origins of Fat Phobia*, American beauty and diet culture is based on this kind of racialized body and style policing and has been for centuries. There's no way to get dressed or prepare for a job interview without getting entangled in this ongoing history.

What this means, among many other things, is that not everyone can get away with being a frump. Depending on who's wearing them and who's viewing them, frumpy styles can come across as:

- This person is rejecting glamour on principle or stylishly participating in a cool antifashion fashion trend.
- This person is poor, depressed, clueless, and/or insecure.

- This person is an entitled asshole who doesn't respect others enough to dress up for them.
- This person is invisible.

Race, class, gender, size, age, employment status, disability status, accent: all of these affect the ways we present ourselves to the world and the ways we're perceived. Being able to be frumpy in public without negative consequences is not an option for everyone.

And frump is not an option that everyone wants. Insofar as frumpiness is the sartorial equivalent of unseasoned food, it can be an unappealing and even oppressive aesthetic. For me, frump might feel like a comfortable invisibility cloak. To others, it can feel like a painful erasure. If you belong to a category that glamour has been defined *against*, glamour might not be something that you want to let go.

In her writing about the Supremes and other Black music icons, cultural critic Daphne A. Brooks has invoked "the civil right to Black glamour" as a significant part of the Civil Rights Movement. Fashion journalist Nichelle Gainer celebrates this kind of groundbreaking style in her lavish coffee table volumes, *Vintage Black Glamour* and *Gentlemen's Quarters*, which illustrate how Eartha Kitt, Sidney Poitier, and others have wielded a kind of culture-shaking beauty that reverberates across the decades. For many Black people and people of color, insisting on their own style in a predominantly white and/or frumpy fashionscape has long been a way to defy and navigate structures of racist exclusion, oblivious entitlement, and dubious or absent fashion sense.

Learning this history has helped me better understand the political significance of style choices that I used to think of as mere personal preferences. With hindsight, I can see the racial exclusion in the white professor's email. I can also see the countercultural community-building in my ultrastylish grad school advisor's decision to give all her advisees gift certificates for manicures. She was supporting us and her favorite nail artist, but more than that, she was resisting the oppressive idea that physical adornment is a distraction from the life of the mind. As the first Black woman to get tenure in the department, she was trying to foster a world that made more space for women like herself.

I now also have a better sense of why the program's only Latina faculty member told me so adamantly, "When I went into this profession, I made a decision that I was not taking out my gold hoops for anyone ever." I thought of her when I read Alexandria Ocasio-Cortez's tweet on the day she was sworn into Congress—the perfect rejoinder to white women who give toxic style advice:

Lip+hoops were inspired by Sonia Sotomayor, who was advised to wear neutral-colored nail polish to her confirmation hearings to avoid scrutiny. She kept her red. Next time someone tells Bronx girls to take off their hoops, they can just say they're dressing like a Congresswoman.

I still love frump, but I'm not as comfortable with it as I used to be. Like the mandatory glamour of *Sex and the Single Girl*, it's a flawed response to an impossible situation.

In her famous monologue in *The Devil Wears Prada*, fashion magazine editor Miranda Priestly (Meryl Streep) lectures frumpy assistant Andy Sachs (Anne Hathaway) about how even though

Andy likes to think she's superior to the vapid world of fashion, she's still inevitably participating in it: the color of Andy's lumpy blue sweater can be traced back to the runways of Paris and placed in the context of the global fashion economy.

There's obviously a lot that Miranda's monologue leaves out. Her trickle-down model of fashion ignores the fact that the haute couture designers she references probably borrowed/appropriated this color from stylish people on the street. She also doesn't mention that no matter what Andy wears, she still benefits every day from looking like Anne Hathaway.

However, Miranda is right that even people who don't want to think about glamour are still subject to and complicit in its power, in the workplace and elsewhere. No matter how lumpy our sweater or frumpy our flannel, we remain stuck in global and historical structures that monetize and sometimes weaponize style. In fact, frumpiness can be an evasion of more than just constricting waistbands. It can be a kind of refusal to recognize or reckon with the larger systems we live in and the way they oppress or reward us.

I own a whole rolling rack of clothes that don't fit anymore—a row of vintage dresses that were full of memories even before I got them, and that remind me of all the memories I made in them. For almost two decades now, in whatever apartment I've lived in, the dresses have been in my bedroom, arranged in rainbow order. I see them every day.

For a long time, I've thought about these dresses as a problem to be solved. At first, I thought the best solution was to change my body so I would fit into them again. Later, I thought the best solution was to change my feelings about my body so that I could simply accept that I'd never wear them again and give them away without a qualm.

Now I no longer think about the rolling rack as a solvable problem. Whether or not I wear the dresses again, I'll remain an aging woman in a misogynist world, marked by my battles with beauty culture and my attempts at glamour and frump. No amount of self-discipline or self-love will resolve the dissonance between actual human bodies and the systems that judge and taxonomize them.

And so, you could say I'm practicing "closet positivity": I accept the clothes as a record of who I used to be, which is part of who I am. They are neither siren song nor protest—just old dresses hanging next to my new flannel billowcases.

Girl Meets Purity Culture

Giaae Kwon

If I couldn't go down the heteronormative
path expected of me, I could at least pursue
the second-best thing: celibacy.

I daresay it's typical for single people my age to lose hours of our lives staring at dating apps on our phones, tapping through photos, swiping left or right, but I can't say I enjoy doing it (does anyone?). Part of me feels obligated, though, to put myself out there and try to find love. I'm in my midthirties, after all. I've been single my whole life. I've never dated, never been kissed or had sex.

In another world, the one in which I was raised, my chastity would be a source of pride. My former church leaders might point to me as an example: *Look how pure she is. May God bless her with a husband to help fulfill her purpose!* Of course, this would be a gross misinterpretation of my comfort with being single, but that doesn't matter—I'm no longer in that world. In fact, I've spent the last five years trying to shake it.

The message from my Korean Presbyterian church was clear: our bodies were temples, vessels of worship whose ultimate purpose was to bring glory to God. For boys, purity culture meant hyping them to be masculine figureheads who would take their rightful place at the heads of their families. Meanwhile, girls were taught to resist the animalistic urges of boys, to save ourselves for marriage—or to remain celibate if we weren't blessed with husbands. While we were expected to excel in everything we did, including school and careers, we were also meant to follow the model of our religious leaders: marry young, have lots of babies (birth control was considered a form of abortion), then homeschool our children while our husbands supported us financially and led us in the ways of Christianity.

In short, our bodies were not ours. They belonged in service to our husbands and children—and, through them, to God.

Purity culture dovetailed neatly with the body-shaming that began in high school, which came from every corner of my community: family, friends, random ajummas (middle-aged women) at restaurants who had no problems voicing opinions on how I looked and what I was eating. Korean culture is communal, one in which the social unit overrides the individual. This means your shame is your family's shame, and it leaves you wide open to other Koreans openly conveying their judgments and opinions about you. I was regularly ridiculed, called names, scathingly told at every meal to stop eating—I'd had enough, wasn't I full yet? It hit harder, more cruelly, because it was always masked in care: *We say this because we love you, and we know others will reject you.*

Born in New York City to 1.5-generation Korean parents (meaning they immigrated when they were young), I grew up in Los Angeles surrounded predominantly by Koreans. From a young age, I was held to Korean body standards, which start with thinness: a body must first be thin to have a chance at being considered acceptable, pretty, or desirable. My body—supposedly still a holy vessel, just one that needed to be corrected—felt doubly re-moved from me.

For over fifteen years, I tried to hide myself away in dark clothing, avoided socializing, and waited for my life to start, whenever that day might come. I jumped from diet to diet, exer-cised obsessively, and logged every calorie I consumed. My body was a leaden thing: it couldn't feel; it couldn't want. But more than that, my body was one that *shouldn't* feel. I had no need for desire, and though desire never factored into the religious teachings I grew up with, I implicitly understood that some kind of basic at-traction was required for a successful marital coupling—which, after all, was a woman's divine purpose. At that, my undesirable body failed. Even if I let myself indulge in that kind of yearning, my logic went, who would want me? And if my body was an affront to those around me, did it have any value to God?

It would be wiser, then, to resolve myself to a life of purity and singlehood, I reasoned. If I couldn't go down the heteronormative path expected of me, I could at least pursue the second-best thing: celibacy.

Today, I know that my body is fairly average and always has been, allowing me to move mostly unfettered through the West-ern world, but my body dysmorphia, developed over many long years, continues to be so severe that I don't believe it. Half a life-time of shaming will do that to a person—break them down until they no longer feel whole, instead just a bunch of limbs that are all wrong.

And yet, as strange as this sounds, body-shaming served a

kind of twisted purpose in my life. I shouldn't have had to experience so much trauma in order to avoid another form of trauma, but it's true: body-shaming insulated me from the direct impact of purity culture because none of my church leaders worried that I was in danger of being sexually deviant. I was the "good girl," the studious one who was more concerned with getting into college and eventually law school than going to parties and meeting boys. My kind of ambition was acceptable by both church and Korean standards; it didn't mean I'd *never* find a godly man to marry and have children with, if that was God's plan for me.

Because my body supposedly removed me from temptation by rendering me undesirable, I got my purity education mostly by proxy. Friends at church were busy crushing on boys, sneaking out of their houses to make out in public parks. Sometimes they'd come to service with hickeys or rumors of bad behavior. I watched as they were pulled aside and sternly lectured, while I sat passively by in our gender-segregated Bible studies.

Even if I wanted to be a typical teenager like my friends, I don't know that I could have carried the additional burden of believing myself impure; I was already splintering from the body-shaming and wracked with self-hatred, so I felt almost proud of being a "good Christian girl." Our church leaders didn't have to pull *me* aside; I was an example to my boy-crazy friends. It didn't matter then that my so-called purity was the result of shutting myself off from my body, from desire. I didn't care at all.

When I was twenty years old, I learned that some women shave "down there." I don't remember how I came across this fact, but I was instantly intrigued. It seemed like such a strange and scandalous thing to be so intimately familiar with one's "private parts" and to think about how they might feel to yourself or appear to someone else.

After a cursory Google search, I headed to Target. I'd never shaved any part of my body before; my mother taught me to use an epilator to remove the hair from my legs and armpits because that's what she did. I found myself overwhelmed by all the options—what was the difference between a shaving cream and a shaving gel? What made a decent razor? Why was everything Pepto-Bismol pink? In the end, I opted for whatever seemed the most basic and scurried back to my apartment, glad that my roommate was in lab all day, and locked myself in our shared bathroom. I peeled off my pants and underwear and perched myself on the cold ledge of the bathtub.

I froze.

Was I supposed to *look* first? I'd never *looked* before. I'd also never actually touched myself, other than as a quick part of my shower routine. Eventually, I got up to fetch a hand mirror, placed it on the ledge, and angled it between my legs. I couldn't bring myself to really look; it felt vulgar to see what my vaginal area looked like. I fumbled my way through the shaving process, somehow figuring out how to apply the foamy cream, pull my skin taut, and shave away my pubic hair. Frankly, it was a miracle I didn't cut myself as I shaved all the way down, leaving only a lopsided triangle, because why try at all if you aren't going to commit?

As it turned out, shaving my vulva was a terrible idea. It was nice at first, when my skin was soft and smooth, but the next day, as soon as the tiniest bit of growth started, the irritation felt unbearable.

I started masturbating by accident, as a way to soothe my sandpaper skin. Holding my legs apart and introducing some kind of lubrication was the only thing that delivered any kind of relief, and it wasn't like I had lube sitting around (or even knew what lube was at the time), so I used what my body, miraculously, produced on its own. For a while, this practice wasn't about pleasure—I didn't know what I was doing, and nothing necessarily felt good, per se.

It just felt curious, because my body was a curiosity. Even at twenty, I was barely familiar with it, and I'd certainly never thought of my body as being capable of pleasure.

Touching myself unfurled little knots of warmth in me, though, and so I kept doing it. My clumsy external stimulation started to feel nice, I thought, but maybe it could be better if I knew what I was doing. I read what I could on the internet and tried fantasizing about scenes from *Sailor Moon* fan fiction, but even then, it wasn't so much about the physical as it was about unlocking different parts of my imagination. The pleasure came from my body, yes, but it was fueled by the fantasies in my brain, thoughts I'd never had before, answering questions about what I wanted, who I wanted, what made me feel good.

When I finally recognized this as masturbation, I felt a secret thrill. I was still going to church and I was still a good Christian girl, but I was also in bed midday with my shades drawn, slipping my hand down my pants, ignoring the voice in the back of my head that said this was wrong. Masturbation was sinful, that much I knew, but I didn't know exactly why. I also didn't care. It was a wonder to me that I was able to feel like this, like my body was lighting up and coming to life in ways I never thought possible. It felt too good to give up because of shame.

Besides, it wasn't like I was having sex with someone else. I was single and celibate, so as far as sins go, I reasoned, this must be a minor one.

Over time, I started to intellectualize my faith-based shame as it mutated into what I thought I *should* feel and do. After all, what good Christian girl orders toys off the internet, reads erotica, learns what gets her off best? Does a good Christian girl lie in bed and fantasize about what sex might be like, then cry after she comes because she's so tired of getting herself off alone? And would a good Christian girl feel shame over her lack of sexual experience, rather than being proud of her purity?

By my midtwenties, I started feeling the weight of my perpetual virginity and singleness. Free from their parents' homes, my friends were out dating, getting laid, and having their hearts broken, while I was still locked in fear, unable to meet new people and put myself out in the world. I didn't know that I wanted someone else to see all of me. My shame took on a new dimension: I was ashamed of my body, yes, but I was also ashamed of having reached this stage of my life without having experienced physical intimacy with someone else.

I learned to stay quiet and listen when my few friends discussed dates, boyfriends, one-night stands, so I wouldn't expose my inexperience. I gave advice based on theoretical speculation on how relationships worked, never offering up anything personal, trying not to draw attention to myself. I was afraid everyone would think there was something wrong with me. For the first time, I wished I was the type of person who could go to a bar, chat someone up, and let myself be taken home, undressed, and touched.

Feeling desire through self-pleasure had begun to unlock something within me, but it would take a move across the country from Los Angeles to New York City—far from the community that taught me shame—before I could admit that I wanted someone to desire me. I finally felt free to probe all the broken parts of myself and began to piece them back together. It took years, but I emerged from my fear and made new friends. I even went speed dating, which led to a few actual dates. I took myself out to nice dinners, book events, and concerts. I learned to enjoy my singlehood.

I wish this story had a straightforward, happy ending: girl is raised in purity culture with Korean beauty standards and learns to hate her body; girl reconnects with herself and discovers her sexuality; girl falls in love, gets laid, and moves on. That would be the rom-com version of my life. Reality, of course, is more complicated.

I'm still single in my midthirties. I haven't been laid; I haven't even been kissed. I'm not embarrassed by any of those facts now, though.

That doesn't mean the loneliness is no longer there, or that I've fully shed shame. Body dysmorphia is still my faithful companion, but underneath that struggle is a daily determination to reclaim my body, to learn pleasure, and—most of all—to find joy in who I am, as I am.

It's no rom-com, but it *is* a happy ending of sorts.

Girl finds her way out of body-shaming and purity culture.

She has no patience for razors, hates waxing, and tweezes her hair now, finding the process relaxing. She knows the parameters of her desire, if not yet the full extent of it. She doesn't care what you think of her singleness, though she does still worry what you think about her looks. But then, even that's okay. Because, for the first time, her body feels alive.

The Animal Within the Animal
Melissa Febos

In solitude, like masturbation, the body
opens—but if not to another, then to what?

After twenty years of consecutive monogamous relationships, I decide to spend three months completely celibate. Technically, I decided this a year ago, but then promptly got into five brief entanglements. Each had a frantic tinge, like the last handful of popcorn you cram into your mouth after you've promised yourself to stop eating it.

Though I'm fairly certain I'm not a "sex and love addict,"[1] I attend a few recovery meetings to confirm it. Changing a fundamental part of one's lifestyle or outlook tends to pull back the veil on unexamined beliefs, and deliberating over what to wear to my first meeting reveals my bias against femme fashion, as opposed to athleisure. I don't want to dress the part; my usual attire—form-fitting head-to-toe black and heels—seems to evoke sex and love

---

1 As distinct from a "sex addict." There are different recovery communities for each.

addict.[2] I decide on the only pair of loose-fitting pants I own, a hoodie, and sneakers.

I've often envied women who wear sneakers every day; perhaps I'll be wearing them, too, by the end of my celibate period. The prospect both excites and scares me. How much of what I consider my personality—clothes look better on me with heels—are symptoms of my orientation to the perceptions of others in general and potential lovers in particular?

On my way to the meeting, I get a text from a recent date. I didn't have a great time with her, but still agreed when she suggested we see each other again partly because I find disagreeing disagreeable, especially when it can be postponed, and partly because I wasn't ready to eliminate the option yet. Hoarding romantic possibilities is an old and reliable source of comfort.

I consider texting her back to explain I'm not interested. I consider telling her that I'll be available in three months. Instead, I put my phone in my pocket.

Though I expected the recovery meeting to be full of straight women who look like wrung-out dish towels, I'm surprised to find the cozy, wood-floored room in the back of the church populated by vivacious women. Plenty of them are dressed all in black and wearing heels. They don't appear to have sold their souls to

---

2 I suspect there are actually more sex addicts clad in athleisure than in all-black and heels, as these styles generally fall along gendered lines, so my bias is probably just a symptom of your run-of-the-mill internalized sexism. (While there are studies that show men are more likely to develop sex addiction, it's also true that men have overwhelmingly made up the subjects of sex addiction studies.)

the god of heterosexual fetishism.[3] A few even emit a queer signal, though all are femme presenting. I sit in a folding metal chair with my Styrofoam cup of coffee, embarrassed by my presumptuousness.

The meeting's speaker talks about never being single, getting off on being wanted by people she wasn't even attracted to, having boyfriends she was ashamed to be seen with in public, compulsively masturbating. She also refers to something called a "rain check," which, as far as I can tell, is when you keep a sexual or romantic option open, just in case, despite it being unappealing or inappropriate. *I always kept the back burner warm*, she tells us.

When she started recovery, she spent a year totally free of dating, sex, flirting, and masturbation. This sounds extreme to me, although before I got clean from heroin, total abstinence from all mind-altering chemical substances also seemed extreme to me.

But then, sex and love lie in a less binary realm of addictions—along with food, work, and codependency—whose objects can't necessarily be removed wholesale from one's life. I gather from the women who share their stories next that every sex and love addict determines their own definition of abstinence, based on their own particular set of troubling behaviors, though many relinquished masturbation.

Once I get over my delight at being in a room of women willing to refer casually to their self-pleasure practices, my resistance is immediate. I hadn't even considered refraining from masturbation. I don't think it's ever been a compulsive behavior for me, except perhaps during puberty, and I'm not interested in patholo-

---

3   Apparently, I think of sex and love addiction as kind of a straight thing (thereby rendering it extra distasteful), which I know isn't true.

gizing healthy behaviors. I've decided to be celibate in an effort to simplify my life, not complicate it.

On the other hand, I'm also here because I don't entirely trust my own perceptions. Compulsive behaviors are resilient and can bend perception to protect themselves. A compulsion that causes anxiety and also treats it can function like a psychological auto-immune disorder.

My first orgasm was to the movie *Valley Girl*, starring Nicolas Cage. I sat on the floor, experimenting with my body, while my grandmother lay asleep behind me on the sofa.

But my first lover was the bathtub faucet.[4] How did I even think to position myself under it, feet flat against the wall on either side of the hot and cold knobs? It wasn't a natural position, but it was a natural inclination.

After that, I experimented with all sorts of household objects and reading materials from *Valley of the Dolls* to *Rubyfruit Jungle*.

How comforting it was to learn, years later, of the "hydrotherapy" craze that took hold of European and North American bath houses in the late eighteenth century. From Bath, England, to Saratoga Springs, New York, doctors touted the water cure for the

---

4   During the writing of this essay, I was continually frustrated by the deficit of synonyms for "masturbation," which is such an ungainly word and occurred so very many times, but all the alternatives were either phallocentric or gross, and most were both. Some alternative options that I solicited from friends: she-bop, winnowing, polishing the pearl, fracking, rubbing one out (I suspect originally intended for those with penises but clearly applies more aptly to clitoral masturbation), flicking the bean, clicking the mouse, handy tooling, jilling off, spackling, and diddling the skittle. I personally came up with "the Circle Game," although it may be too specific to my own masturbatory motions. Eve Kosofsky Sedgwick's "isometric exercise" is also a favorite.

disease of hysteria, which had literally been plaguing women for centuries, according to men.

The word *hysteria* is derived from the Greek word for uterus, which Plato famously described as "the animal within the animal."[5] It was believed that the uterus would set out wandering around the body if it was deprived of a baby, repelled and drawn by powerful smells, like a raccoon poking around a row of garbage cans. Everyone from ancient Greeks to doctors who specialized in gynecology hundreds of years later postulated that a bad case of Wandering Womb led to hysteria, that better-known affliction.

Symptoms might include headaches; fatigue; any sort of melancholy, frustration, or anxiety; an excess or deficit of sexual interest with "an approved male partner"—basically, the expression of any response other than total contentment to the patriarchal structures that governed their lives or a failure to reinforce the androcentric model of sex that reigned (and still does). Doctors of the nineteenth century claimed that more than 70 percent of women suffered from hysteria, thereby making it the pandemic of their time.

Hydrotherapy most popularly featured a high-pressure shower or "douche" that massaged the pelvic region—sometimes in the exact way I discovered my bath faucet could at eleven. According to an 1851 essay by R. J. Lane about an English spa, after treatment the patients often claimed to feel "as much elation and buoyancy of spirits, as if they had been drinking champagne." Common prescriptions suggested application of the water douche

---

5   Centuries later, Sigmund Freud developed the theory of the unconscious mind—the mind within the mind—which he similarly characterized as a sort of wild animal. He also wrote, with the physician Josef Breuer, an entire book about hysteria, *Studies in Hysteria* (published in 1895).

for four to five minutes, the same length of time in which most people are able to achieve orgasm via manual masturbation.

Despite my lack of neurosis around masturbation, I didn't get my first vibrator until my senior year of college, when a friend gifted me a pink Pocket Rocket. A bestseller for some forty years, it's the Toyota of vibrators: unglamorous, reliable, longitudinal. I used it for a decade, until its buzz grew so loud that it sounded like an actual Toyota in need of a new muffler and finally sputtered out for good.

In my early twenties, my best friend and I lived in a series of Brooklyn apartments and shared a gargantuan vibrator that we christened "the Hammer of the Gods." It was roughly the size and shape of a human arm, hinged at the "elbow," with a blunt end where its hand would be. Whenever we felt so moved, we would simply shuffle into the other's room, unplug it, and carry it to our own bedroom. We joked that we practically had to wear jeans when using it because the even the lowest setting would otherwise render our genitals insensate.

The Hammer wasn't what either of us would've chosen (most likely a Hitachi Magic Wand, that more elegant, powerhouse vibrator), but it had been a gift to my roommate from a client at the dungeon where we both worked as pro-dommes. That's also where we met, and where I learned how to talk freely about my own pleasure. When desire (or anything, really) becomes a perfunctory part of one's job, it's stripped of whatever aura it carried before. There's no room for the sacred or profane in shoptalk.

The client who gifted it to us would come in every week for a session with his current favorite, moving on every month or so to a newer hire. His requests were predictable: he basically just wanted to watch you get off with a giant vibrator, or to get you off with it. It seemed like a good deal, getting paid seventy-five dollars an hour to be brought to orgasm, or to masturbate for a one-man audience whose opinion meant next to nothing.

But I saw him only once. I found it unbearable to be watched and couldn't stand to let a strange man do what I so enjoyed doing myself.

It makes sense that men in the nineteenth century wanted the hysteria "solution" to be administrable only by them. They got to have it all: to propagate a model of ideal sex that served them alone in terms of pleasure and procreation, to medicalize women's pleasure, and to encourage women's dependence on them. This way, they could deprive women of the legitimate satisfactions of both social freedom and sexual pleasure, pathologize their natural response, and then charge them money for a modicum of temporary relief. What a coup, for men to convince us that being brought to orgasm only by them was a "cure" for the imaginary illness whose symptoms were our humanity; to tell us that to masturbate ourselves (along with drinking coffee or alcohol, and a slew of other ordinary behaviors) was a cause of the illness.[6]

There's a five-minute break halfway through the recovery meeting. I smile at the other women as I refill my tiny cup with watery

---

6 How appropriate that George Taylor, who patented his steam-powered table vibrator in the late nineteenth century, called the cumbersome and expensive apparatus the "Manipulator."

coffee. I pull out my phone and look at the text from my former date. I put my phone away again.

I can see how breaking the habit of issuing rain checks might be useful. However, the idea of banning masturbation when it hasn't caused a problem stinks a little bit of what Foucault called "the hysterization of women's bodies," which is to say the dangerous and deeply misogynistic practice of pathologizing women's sexuality such that it requires the medical interventions of men.

On the other hand, there are no men here.

Locked inside the bathroom, hazy with steam and the *ssshhhh-hhh* of rushing water, I felt most alone. In the trance of orgasm, I forgot myself completely. I forgot the bath, the room, the house, the town—every context in which I understood myself. Without a self, a body is everywhere and nowhere at once. Pleasure becomes synesthetic—exploding like splattered paint across the sky of consciousness. It's a big bang of deafening thunder, the smell of lavender and salt.

"In this vision my soul, as God would have it, rises up high into the vault of heaven and into the changing sky and spreads itself out," wrote Hildegard von Bingen, the Benedictine abbess and mystic saint who's intrigued me since I was a child. In her seventies, she described her lifelong visions in a letter: "The light which I see . . . is far, far brighter than a cloud which carries the sun. I can measure neither height, nor length, nor breadth in it; and I call it 'the reflection of the living Light.' And as the sun, the moon, and the stars appear in water, so writings, sermons, virtues, and certain human actions take form for me and gleam."

The aloneness of orgasm, the unbeingness of it, is similar in many ways to that of creation. When I am in the trance of creative concentration my self and its external contexts disappear, though sensation persists. The body becomes a mirror that reflects something other than self, something that disperses the self to make room for a different kind of story.

I try to imagine, instead of pursuing my own ecstasy under the rush of water, standing in a bathhouse while doctors hose me down with a massive, deafening contraption.

As an adult, I've not often been a light-candles-around-the-bathtub type of masturbator. I'm more of an eat-a-bag-of-chips kind of masturbator. A procrasturbator. The time that I most reliably masturbate is when I'm in the early stages of writing something new. Maybe it's a way to burn off the nervous energy of breaking ground on a thing, but that seems generous.

The definition of compulsion is an act meant to relieve a mental obsession, or some kind of distress. In that sense, my masturbatory practices qualify as compulsive. I'm compelled by the anxiety of writing to watch a round of porn and have a handful of orgasms.

But then, when lovers asked me to touch myself so they could watch, I always refused. I was shy, but that wasn't it. There was no performance to my self-pleasure and there was so much performance with lovers. Masturbation felt private in a way that made exposure intolerable.

It also seemed like the only kind of sex that had nothing to do with pleasing anyone else or performing my desire or sexuality for someone else's benefit. As a young person, it felt in direct opposition to my partnered experiences. Though I've had plenty of orgasms with other people in my twenties and thirties, there was always an element of performance, of body consciousness, of other orientation. But the pleasure of a solitary orgasm has often felt like sunlight or thunder—elemental.

I'd had no internalized male gaze that directed my masturbation, and not because self-pleasure is exempt from it; it forms the basis of a whole genre of porn, with copious subgenres. My masturbatory fantasies abound with all sorts of hyperpatriarchal shit, but those images don't dominate my consciousness or govern what I do with my body. I suspect that this exemption is due to the fact that my practice of self-pleasure predates that of performance. It's a relationship I formed with myself before I ever formed a sexual relationship with another person.

And so, my need for celibacy has more to do with performance than it does with pleasure. It's not physical lust that's compelled me from monogamous relationship to monogamous relationship. If my ceaseless entanglements are a result of the ways that I relate to other people, then the goal of my celibacy is to relate to myself.

When Hildegard von Bingen took a vow of celibacy, her ostensible goal was to relate more closely to God. But God didn't assume human form; the only human forms in her abbey were other women, and she worked her whole life to make it so. At their inductions, she dressed them as brides in extravagant white silk, their hair flowing long and wild. She even had passionate relationships with some—though according to her, she never had sex with anyone.

How then, did she write the first description of a female orgasm? How did she know the "sense of heat in her brain"? How "the woman's sexual organs contract, and all the parts that are ready to open up during the time of menstruation now close, in the same way as a strong man can hold something enclosed in his fist"?

Beguine Mechthild of Magdeburg writes of eating and drinking Christ in sensuous rapture, while Beguine Agnes Blannbekin tells a bizarre story of conjuring the foreskin of Christ on her tongue and swallowing it, an act that wracks her whole body with orgasmic pleasure, one she repeats a hundred times. Catherine of Siena used Christ's foreskin as a ring when she wed him. Teresa of Ávila writes of an angel who "plunged [his] dart several times into my heart and that it reached deep within me. When he drew it out, I thought he was carrying off with him the deepest part of me; and he left me all on fire with great love of God. The pain was so great that it made me moan, and the sweetness this greatest pain caused me was so super-abundant that there is no desire capable of taking it away."

Some of these descriptions read like straightforward erotica, sometimes quite kinky and seemingly stripped of coy metaphors. Others, like the accounts of Hildegard, seem more to convey oneness with the world, a spiritual experience achieved through the body (as so many are).

It's also a recurrent theme in hip-hop. As Tyler the Creator raps in Pusha T's "Trouble on My Mind," *I'm a problem / 'Cause I wanna fuck the world but not a fan of using condoms*. Like many rappers, his is less an erotic wish than one of domination. He wants to overpower the world, maybe even impregnate it, as fucking and impregnating a woman would be evidence of his masculinity and dominance.[7]

---

7   Similarly, *go fuck yourself* is one of the more satisfying insults, though it
    doesn't make a lot of sense to me. Who doesn't want to go fuck themselves?
    Some of the best fucking of my life has been with myself.

Conversely, the female mystics want to *yield* to the divine, to disperse their selfhood into the universe. Though I want to be careful not to reinforce a false binary: men want to dominate while women want to yield. We are powerfully conditioned in these relationships to sex—socially, legally, and in all the more insidious ways. However it assigns power, it is a dichotomy that harms everyone. I imagine what it must feel like to have your sex, your very genitals, equated with dominance and violence, an insult[8] equated with defilement, and it must be confusing, degrading in a different but not incomparable way to having euphemisms for my genitals used as an insult equated with weakness.[9]

I suspect that everyone has desires to yield and to dominate. Sometimes, even the mystic saints' descriptions of yielding sound nothing like submission. When the divine is writing through you, your voice might sound more like that of a god than a supplicant. Most of us find imaginative means of articulating even our most stigmatized desires. Sometimes wanting to fuck the world must be expressed in more poetic terms.

"I am the flame above the beauty in the fields," wrote Hildegard. "I shine in the waters; I burn in the sun, the moon, and the stars. And with the airy wind, I quicken all things vitally by an unseen, all-sustaining life."

At the summer camp I attended as an adolescent, we played a game called Fishbowl, during which all the girls would sit in a circle

---

8   "Eat a dick," "suck my dick," "fuck you," and on and on, ad infinitum.

9   How disturbing and sad it is that our genitals are so often the basis of our most poisonous insults.

while the boys sat silently outside of it (in a following round, we would reverse positions). A female counselor would ask questions that the boys had submitted anonymously ahead of time. One of the questions the boys always asked was, *What does a female orgasm feel like?*

Convulsion, we said.

A bright light flashing. A ripe persimmon, squeezed in a fist.

Hildegard called her work "the living light." She told others of her visions starting in her early childhood, but no one particularly cared until she was forty. As soon as her direct line to God was recognized by men, she claimed that God had commanded her: "Make known the wonders you live, put them in writing, and speak."

In the High Middle Ages, women weren't allowed to write music in the Church, and certainly no one was interested in their ideas or stories—but Hildegard became one of the most powerful and prolific thinkers in history. She wrote copious religious and scientific texts, was an unparalleled composer and lyricist, and even invented a secret language for her nuns to speak to one another.

Her understanding of physical pleasure seems not to have hindered this, though I think entanglement with another person certainly would have.

I decide that I can masturbate in my period of celibacy. This abstinence is all about other people, not the expulsion or containment of desire. Solitude, I believe, can be very sexy. In solitude, like masturbation, the body opens—but if not to another, then to what?

When I get home from the meeting, I look at the text from my date once more. Then I delete it and block her number.

Afterward, there's an empty feeling that reminds me of turning off the television as a kid. As if all the light has momentarily been sucked out of the room. There's a flutter of terror—*What now?*

But I can hear the hum of the refrigerator, a car hissing by outside. My own breath rises and falls.

Perhaps the mystic nuns just wanted to live freely among other women, to compose music and write and wear luxurious silks and let their hair flow freely. Proving an exceptional relationship to God was the single route to such freedoms. Yielding to the divine was the only way to avoid yielding to men.

I don't think desire to be free precludes a relationship to the divine, or that either precludes erotic pleasure. The body is an instrument for all of these, but in every case, its retrieval from the possession of others is a first step.

Alone in my bedroom, I touch myself and think of the universe. As pleasure disperses my consciousness, I can feel the world getting bigger.

Self-Help
Morgan Parker

With any luck, correctly calculating my score will
illuminate the long-elusive question posed by men in
my bed and kind old ladies alike: *Why are you single?*

I've never read a self-help book before. I don't like when people
tell me what to do, and I really hate when they're telling everyone
else the same thing. Yet here I am, earnestly and soberly poring
over a quiz in a self-help book about relationships, which I actually spent money on because I'm thirty-three years old and I've
been single my entire life.

Not single "for a long time," but single forever, the whole time.
Single may not even be the right word, because absence implies a
memory of what once took its place. I'm single the way a baby is
single.

By most sociocultural standards established since the beginning of time, my adult life could be viewed as inadequate and incomplete, if not tragic.

One thing about being unhappily single in your thirties—besides
the very real biological and social pressure to reproduce—is ev-

erybody thinks there must be a reason why. A reason that you must be somewhat content with or aware of, if you're taking no steps to improve your situation. As long as a person is unhappily single, there must be something wrong. You must need help.

Everyone has an opinion, whether I ask for it or not. Even strangers assume the authority to spit out armchair wisdom about what I need to do, acknowledge, let go of; how to get out of my comfort zone or "be open" or whatever. Because, of course, it's the task of the single person to receive and carry out any instruction from self-help books, magazines, friends, coworkers, mothers, people on buses, seminars, cab drivers, etc.

When it's not friends or Uber drivers with hollow clichés and prepackaged, one-size-fits-all advice, it's middle-aged businessmen at hotel bars or chatty randoms on airplanes with the gall to throw the question at me, shaking their heads like I'm a math problem. Sometimes it's people I'd hoped might be interested themselves, men who would go on to kiss or sleep with me, and even those who'd already done so.

"Why are you single?" they press, in disbelief or suspicion, rattling off my many fantastic qualities.

Rarely am I speechless. But I never have a witty quip in response to this question, and the words *you tell me* feel like glass shards leaving my throat. "Slavery, white women," I replied once. Another time, on what I'd foolishly thought to be a date, I pressed my palms to the table and announced, "I believe I am the least desirable woman in America."

"I'm just not in a good place for a relationship right now," they say, before starting one with somebody else a week later. One such man lamented to me that he was an *anxious avoidant* personality. Usually, they're just hung up on their exes.

When white guys say it, I hate that I have to wonder if they're also trying to avoid the reality of actually having a Black girlfriend—bringing her home to the family in Maryland or Milwaukee; potentially adjusting the makeup of his social life; becoming compelled, as if possessed, to blurt out, "My girlfriend's Black," in defense, or as confession, explanation, excuse.

"You deserve someone better," they say. But "I'm not good enough for you" is just another way of making the rejection feel like my fault. No one answers the question.

I mentioned the *anxious avoidant* terminology to my psychiatrist, the one who's always telling me to go on dates, and who's been trying to steer me away from "young men who are artist types." She recommended this book on "attachment styles" and explained how the authors suggest that people are either anxious, secure, or avoidant in relationships. She said I'm attracting the wrong attachment style. So I bought the self-help book and endeavored to read it.

I barely skim the intro, guiltlessly gliding over the authors' case studies about their friends—Pam's low self-esteem, Sam's obsession with his ex, Eli's boredom with his marriage—but when I read the bulleted list of each attachment style's tendencies, my throat drops to my stomach: every column's unhealthy patterns and self-sabotaging behaviors ring uncomfortably true. In lime-green pen I write *lol* next to a short paragraph on the "rare combination of attachment anxiety and avoidance," a category that "only a small percentage of the population falls into," because it describes 99 percent of my dating pool. You can find *anxious avoidant* people, me included, among most "artist types," especially the young men.

I know what you're thinking.

"Have you tried the apps?"

Everyone offers examples of happily committed app users, sometimes including themselves. Even people who don't know what the apps are suggest I try the apps. People love the apps.

I created my first online dating profile fresh out of college and still hopeful, curled up on a curb-salvaged loveseat in the funeral home for mice that was my Avenue C apartment. My roommate, who worked in fashion, told me it was an "instant confidence booster." After ten years and countless starts and stops—including profiles ghostwritten by expert friends and even a full-year premium membership at no small cost, albeit subscribed to by an accidental slip of the thumb—I've formally decided I hate the apps.

My thing about the apps: they make me feel terrible about myself. Like I'm back in middle school. Like I'm watching *The Bachelor* or whatever reality show it is, with all the white women standing in a line being desired. Like I've felt too many times before.

Once something becomes a cultural phenomenon—a mode of communication, an economic system—it begins to feel necessary, and not engaging with it means risking detachment or ostracization. For this and other reasons, including smoking bans on planes, I hate living when I do, and hope eternal for a more suitable placement in my next lifetime.

In order even to be considered eligible for courtship, you have to first be good at taking pictures of yourself on a phone, which projects your face back at you, taunting. You would be judged only by this snapshot of yourself, conveying just a hint of a personality—careful! Not too much!—and a level of sex appeal on par with that of an "Instagram model," whatever that is.

It's not just that there's no smoking on planes, it's also those little pictures of cigarettes slashed through with a hard red line, glaring at me from every surface. The reminder of restriction.

I hate taking pictures of myself on my phone. I don't care to spend time staring back at myself in reverse, practicing a face. Instead, I'm good with words, and I've tried to develop my awkward version of in-person charm—what one reader called "a quirky and relatable vibe."

Vibes and words on dating profiles are secondary at best and might go unread entirely. There's no point in fretting over authenticity when most of the messages you receive just say *hey, how's your day going?* copied and pasted with no personalization or effort required, like being seduced by a greeting card that's blank inside.

The About Me doesn't matter because "bored, might delete" would perfectly suffice; and the standard template on both ends is little more than *I'm just a regular girl, I love music, food, and staying fit! Down for an afternoon hike and a craft beer?* ☺

Nothing against the regular girl, whom I probably know and love—and either way, she's by all cultural standards happier than I am. She gets to relax, check off the boxes of adulthood, certain of her worth and beauty.

When my Avenue C roommate purged her closet of outdated fashions, my side of the foldable clothing rack reaped the spoils. "Are you sure?" I asked as she gleefully dropped more hangers into my arms: blazers, sweater dresses, jumpsuits. Shoulder pads, she said, would never come back in style.

I'm not *just a regular girl*. I don't really want to be. But I want what she has, what she seems to so easily get.

The *Why are you single?* conundrum has sidled up easily to the shame I've felt about the ugly sides of my depression, which piggybacked nicely on the isolation of growing up a weird Black girl in a traditional white suburb. It's not like I needed any extra encouragement to discipline and punish my every flaw, everything that makes me different, anything that someone else might not like about me.

How would I act or even feel, were there no movies or self-help studies or think pieces teaching me how, teaching all of us the same *how*, telling us what to desire?

I'm a scholar of my surface-level self-esteem stuff and the African American self-esteem stuff, the consequences of an unconventional artist lifestyle, being *intimidating*, fearing commitment and abandonment and intimacy and rejection—basically all the fears. I understand my culpability and self-sabotage. (Additionally, it cannot be overstated how impactful the transatlantic slave trade and its resulting political and economic values has been in determining the results of my love life.)

After cycling through so many feelings of unworthiness and insecurity; scaling mountains of hard-won revelations about racism, gender performance, and triggers from childhood; acknowledging my bitterness and letting go of hang-ups both interpersonal and sociopolitical, I've become as psychologically, emotionally, and physically available as I've ever been.

I've been Girl with Impossibly High Standards, Girl Who Puts Career First, Girl Who Self-Sabotages Out of Fear, Girl Who Needs to Love Herself First and Girl Who Gets in Her Own Way, Girl with Unresolved Questions About Sexuality, Girl with Unhealthy Trauma-Based Defenses. I've lived and shed every rom-com protagonist's problems.

There's a cultural assumption that as soon as you've worked those things out, you find your person and start making a family/household/life. Until then, you're not ready, and you're tasked with headbutting and knocking down each internal issue, no matter how much it hurts or how unfair it is that you must assess, Valentine's Day after Valentine's Day, what's wrong about your body or "energy" or psychology or vocabulary or life choices.

Surely not even half the people who've been in love have endured such extensive and unceasing analysis. It seems other people quit critical self-assessment as soon as they're seriously partnered, and instead assume the authority to assess what's wrong with me and the life choices I've made. Unlike me, they have a piece of paper someone signed, promising not to freak out and leave when they're having a bad mental health day.

Before I've seen such commitment with my own eyes, how can I be sure?

Until you've been in love, until you've had your heart broken, there's a large portion of popular culture that's sung at a pitch you can't hear. I can't sit through an episode of *Sex and the City* without spiraling into a fervent scree about expectations of femininity and pointing out oppressive value systems; I argue aloud with romance subplots talkin' 'bout, "See, if I were Julianna Margulies, no way George Clooney would . . ." or whatever, fuming, until every story is the story of what I am lacking.

Lately, even true crime pisses me off, because even serial killers on death row are managing to fall in love left and right. I can't stop thinking about how many chances for plots I've missed, and how I'd never wear that or put up with that, and that must be the reason I'm alone.

I went through high school without a boyfriend; college without a boyfriend or girlfriend; my twenties without cohabitation or postbreakup Ben & Jerry's; no sloppy one-night stands at a bar in Williamsburg or a club on the Lower East Side turned into anything more. As years go by, narrative after narrative evades me; the possible storylines and adventures dwindle and little gasps of optimism deflate, and deflate, and deflate.

There is a difference between being single in your thirties and being "still single" in your thirties. Even I get turned off by restaurants on Seamless with no reviews and none of the stars colored in. Not worth the risk when there are so many other options with rave reviews and familiar names.

I know it's not like I missed my chance or anything, but part of me mourns the love stories that could've been.

What I mean is: I've grown up from a lonely girl into an alone woman.

The attachment style quiz is the main appeal of the self-help book for me, a former straight-A student happy to be given a tangible task, instead of "practice being more open." In spite of steadfast doubt that I'll be in any way transformed by the book's theories, I catch a gust of excitement at the prospect of righting the wrong of my style, the promise of becoming secure and even potentially attracting a secure person.

In chapters 3 and 4, the authors promise a two-step process for determining my attachment style and that of my partner. I skip the worksheet asking me to list examples from past relationships, and the whole chapter about the partner, triggered and ashamed that I can't even advance to step two. I sternly tell myself to discard the feeling that I'm automatically disqualified, beyond help.

My most comparable experience to real relationships is *situationships*. So, not nothing. But kind of nothing. I satisfy my sexual needs by waiting around for "hanging out" to turn into drunk, which then turns into "hooking up"—or, simply put, I have sex with my friends. Ours is a generation that thrives on vagueness, whatever gives us the most leeway in the end. We don't go on dates, we "hang out"; we despise labels.

None of the authors' case studies depict someone in this labelless predicament, devoid of exes altogether. I scan my heart's memories, searching for any dalliance that might, with the right embellishment, suffice as data, at least for these purposes.

I've briefly entertained infrequent and ill-fated possibilities for romance, but one could convincingly classify all these instances as flings or one-night stands or some variation/combination thereof—flirtations I knew wouldn't work out but irrationally hoped might finally be my romantic storyline. Growing up I was the guys' "closest girl friend," first by default, as the less desirable option than the white girl, then when I realized there was little hope in escaping the platonic identity. At least I could delude myself into imagining a *Will-they-or-won't-they?* plot brewing three layers below reality. There are a lot of movies with romantic narratives like this, so probability-wise, the friend zone isn't the absolute worst place to hang out.

Situationships are just wax fruits in a bowl: they look like the real thing until you try to taste.

I take the attachment style quiz like it's the fucking SAT, reading and rereading every statement, hounding myself to be truthful (how much would I care if I saw my date checking out someone else, *really*?), counting and recounting and crossing things out. I even put it down and return to it days later with fresh eyes.

This is the kind of thing I choose to take seriously or assume that I must. With any luck, correctly calculating my score will illuminate the long-elusive question posed by men in my bed and kind old ladies alike: *Why are you single?*

I've been genuinely trying to "be open" and "put myself out there." I go to bars alone like it's my job, and I even look around, resisting the glow of my phone and merely pretending to read. But what I've found is nobody is interested in looking at anyone, not right away, not by any means of effort. At least not at me. What I've found are people scrolling Tinder. In the bar. Right next to a single person. Never making contact, not even to say, *hey, how's your day going?*

In real life, no handsome stranger reaches for the same bell pepper in the produce section, no glances are exchanged in bookstore aisles, no martini appears "from the gentleman at the end of the bar." Everyone is terrible, and putting yourself out there really means putting yourself into the phone, where someone might actually be looking.

It's a tie: five points in the anxious category; five points in secure. In the avoidant category, one point.

I believe my singleness should be considered a community issue; that anyone who knows and regularly interacts with me should be as equally invested in my struggle-search for love. But since the apps became ubiquitous, nobody sets you up.

And though a lot of my friends met their person before app-based dating was seemingly the only option, it's the first thing they suggest. In fact, most of them have relationship histories already, and haven't been listening to this same song uninterrupted for three whole decades, so it's very frustrating that in a time of such peculiar crises as mine, they should have the gall to recommend something they wouldn't do in a million years. I know because occasionally I've responded to coupled friends' "You should try the apps" bullshit by indignantly thrusting my phone at them and have seen their faces as they toss it facedown on the table after just a few quick swipes.

It's much easier (read: effortless) to blurt the name of an app you saw on a commercial than to ponder who might be eligible, let alone reach out to facilitate a setup. Personally, I wonder why they'd rather me meet a stranger on the internet with a one-line About Me, who could be a murderer or rapist or regular old white supremacist, than to suggest a mediocre date with a mediocre guy from their office cafeteria. At least I'd know he's a proper human, and if I disappeared, they'd have a lead.

In our early twenties, singleness was a community issue. We took our responsibility as wingpersons moderately seriously, prioritizing locations where we might meet potential mates, scanning rooms and doing a lap around the dance floor for prospects.

This is no longer the goal of the collective. It's just my problem. I am nobody's responsibility.

Something else about the apps: They're like a whole fucking part-time job. Apparently, you have to consistently put in several hours a week, otherwise you won't even show up on anybody's radar.

As if. I could write four whole books with all that time, and have.

Another game-changing storyline I missed is meeting someone before I became a "public figure" (i.e., on Wikipedia).

As I chose poetry readings over clubs, blazers over party tops, I was aware on a surface level that I was guilty of "putting my career first" and risking prospects. I sort of expected to be in the musical-chairs conundrum I'm in, feeling like I missed an important window. But I didn't realize that by the time I was ready for a relationship, I wouldn't be just a "person" anymore, that I'd have another incarnation.

I'm "out there," everywhere, a lot. According to several unhelpful opinions, that's part of the problem. Flaunting a gregarious stage presence has done little to quash my problem of being "intimidating," feedback I first received at age twelve.

If you're an artist in front of an audience, your best bet is to take whatever you already are and make it extra, be yourself to the extreme. In dating, the opposite is advised. Apparently, you're not supposed to put it all out there at once. I find this vehemently counterintuitive, if not insulting.

It would be impossible for me to mind the traditional rules about stuff you're not supposed to say on a first date, since I say it all the time to audiences across the country. I'm just not in the habit of being demure or mysterious. What's the point of a slow reveal, if my whole job is going around talking about how sad I am, blowing off any opportunity to be coy or cutesy? I think that's why I find even the idea of dating boring. Who has the time to pretend to be one person, then hope your partner doesn't notice you slowly morphing into another, more complicated, and less shiny version?

In the absence of real intimacy, without proper experience or acceptance of it, I've practically professionalized vulnerability—to my assistance, and to my detriment.

To one of the standard OkCupid profile prompts, *The most private thing I'm willing to admit*, I answer, *is probably already accessible on the internet*. If you Google me, one of the first things that comes up is a personal essay detailing how many antidepressants I take.

By now, my destructive patterns are obvious. It's easier for me to hear *no* and dismiss it than to wait for *yes*. Men tell me they're unavailable or unfit, yet obviously I pursue them, virtually begging them to make out as soon as "un-" is uttered, as soon as I know it won't work. Traditional, practical dating rituals are so much less interesting than the outcomes of wild, destined, and illuminating love, or the opportunity for more self-loathing and sticky emotional conundrums.

Conventional dating practices might actually lead to something promising, and what then?

My primary skills of adulthood concern survival and salvage: cleaning up after my every innocent blunder; "figuring it out"; embodying man, woman, and child of the household. Flipping from one to another quicker than a code switch. To an extent, I'm incapable of imagining how I might fare or function in a couple. What if I'm too far behind, too embittered or untrusting?

Sometimes, consoling or debating a potential-love-interest-in-my-imagination about his Actual Relationship, or anxieties or philosophy books or trauma, I'm aware that this guy's being someone he isn't or can't be with his current partner (who's usually of the Carefree White Girl variety). I wonder if that makes me immediately less desirable, not sexy—knowing them on that level. Being real.

I'm not the one they choose to make official. I've never been wanted enough to be. I've also, consciously or not, chosen not to be.

Both the problem and appeal of nonrelationship relationships is that they remove any responsibility from the deal. A foolhardy attempt to resist narrative and do away with the consequences of linearity.

Part of me is romanced by these terms. There is safety in

clinging to the options of only wild and sticky, in being the one to make things difficult for myself before anybody else can.

You give: blow jobs, compliments, hours of unpaid emotional labor. You get what you get.

I have a good life. Though it's caused inordinate grief in my daily existence, my continued and seasoned identity as Single Woman in this socioeconomic situation—as my life becomes more complicated and ambitious—has required me to get creative about my definitions of romance, of fulfillment, of growth. It's required me to reinterpret community and capacity. To be strong in surprising ways.

I am loved and cared for by a close family and warm, inspiring friends. I have my platonic "husbands"—a group of fourteen diverse in race, gender, orientation, and actual marital status—who've committed to me at least in title, and to whom I'm willing to commit and call my people. In the absence of the real thing, and because I've found it is necessary.

I see how it could be easy to overlook just how handy another person is. Just how many large or small gestures that make all the difference in avoiding misfortune: missed flights, that last drink, losing your phone (a bunch of times), keeping plants watered, getting somewhere on time. Not to mention affection and, frankly, regular sex. I'm certain that as a partnered woman I'd receive far more respect from strangers and especially Black elders. I'd be safer.

I was taught that *Miss* and *Ms.* were placeholders until one grew up into *Mrs.* Traditional American family value systems are always in the backs of our minds. Even when we insist they've been transcended, even if we pledge a life of defiance against them, they still define how things are "supposed to be."

The bylaws of American capitalism never meant for me, a descendent of slaves, to be a rights-holding citizen, or for me as a woman to be financially independent(ish). I've burst through several systemic barriers that should have left me dead or destitute by now. And in the same way, the social structure that adjusted itself to American capitalism is meant to favor the heteronormative patriarchal unit.

On a practical level, I'm less equipped than my cohabitating and committed peers to achieve the markers of successful and respectable adulthood; to meet all expectations without significant loss or charitable assistance. These are things I have a feeling my paired-off friends don't take into consideration when evaluating the appropriateness of my incessant despair. While you don't need a partner to be happy, coupledom is assumed to be an integral part of adult life and essential for anyone with too much ambition and not enough serotonin.

If, for example, I'm traveling as a Black woman with more than two suitcases, as I often am. If I forget to drink a glass of water all day. If two people are required for assembly. When sometimes, on tour in another city, I realize no other person in the world has any idea where I am or what I am doing, and nobody needs to. If I am so depressed I can't pull myself from bed to take the dog out. If I am depressed.

If I am depressed, and I think: Who would want this mess to bear? Why would anyone take this on, and wouldn't it be too much to ask of a co-parent, and would it even be responsible to reproduce or build a family, considering the hazard?

Sometimes, I'll just refuse to care for myself, in protest. Just to display how incapable I am, how unreasonable it is to expect one person to be so casually adept at so many things at the exact same time.

A text notification says the number of gun owners nationally has doubled, and those who already had guns are buying more, many citing civil unrest and racial tensions as their inspiration.

The next alert tells me my OkCupid account has been deleted due to inactivity. I didn't even know that could happen.

The problem is time. It shouldn't matter, but it does. Time means regret. Regret means self-punishment. It's not just the general embarrassment of having the romantic subplot of my movie being introduced so late into act 2, it's also the close-fitting sense that time runs out faster for women like me.

What if I die before getting a look at myself in the bright mirror that is partnership, before tasting what everybody's talking about? Before finding somewhere to pour this devotion I've stored up, all this romance I've accumulated and dreamed? I'm a poet who's never experienced true romantic love; I believe this is an American tragedy.

When I go on strike against myself, nobody is there to see the display. No one rescues me, because I'm not a damsel. I can only care for myself by myself.

These days, stillness is the new hustle, the new collective goal. I'm just as tired as we all are, just as ready to exhale. I fantasize about moving to the Valley, a suburb outside the city—settling into the aloneness I know so well, before it's too late to get comfortable at all.

Nobody wants a single artist living at the end of their suburban cul-de-sac, front porch blasting Fela in the morning and wafting weed smoke in the afternoon. Planned communities have no tables for one. Protection is built that way.

I am a thirty-three-year-old single Black female, self-employed, mentally ill, foulmouthed and politically radical. I can't move just anywhere. My safety is never in my control. My comfort isn't guaranteed.

While it doesn't invalidate my successes, the inability to achieve this one life goal—to "find love"—casts a little sorrow on the others. Even major achievements have a sour aftertaste. The more exciting things get, the more disappointed I am. Without a witness, a stakeholder, a rock—why bother?

If one is always in wait of one's Great Love, if every story depends upon this arc, how am I to be proud of the life I've created, who I've let myself become? When am I allowed to get comfortable, feel grown? If I choose to keep hoping for a romantic plot twist, does that render my story incomplete, still a pulsing cursor? And if I settle down, officially give up fretting over profile pages and wanting more from my flings and situations, would it be resignation?

Sometimes it hurts to think about, but then I just write another book, masturbate, cry, complain on Twitter, write another book.

I'm bored of being lonely. I've whined about it, gotten good at it, made it useful. I've learned and lived with my heart, the emotional sting of yearning. But there's still lack, and difficulty. There's still danger, everywhere.

The self-help book collects dust on a nightstand under an inspirational-type book from my other therapist, the one who's always telling me to "maybe just start thinking about possibly going on dates." We don't talk about loneliness anymore. Mostly, we talk about fear.

My life is a good one.

I don't want to keep it to myself.

Once, a White Guy
Tiana Clark

Was my body always a Black body, or only when it had a
white boy in high relief? Could it ever be just a body?

Once, a white guy I dated asked to see my brown beauties. It was
high school, and I barely knew what my body could do. But on my
best friend's water bed, I felt the plastic undulation of the rolling
mini tide swell, so I lifted my shirt the way one lifts a veil—except I
didn't feel precious or expectant underneath. I felt othered and ex-
posed, inspected by the microscope of his eyes. I was worried about
the circumference of my cinnamon-colored areolae. He kissed and
licked and played with my chest for what seemed like an hour. Were
these my brown beauties? Or were they just boobs? Were my breasts
also Black like me? Was my body always a Black body, or only when
it had a white boy in high relief? Could it ever be just a body?

Once, a white guy pulled my weave so hard during sex that the
thread broke across the woven track. I'd warned him to be careful
with me.

Once, a white guy said my lips felt like large pillows after we kissed.

Once, a white guy I was fucking asked me to make corn bread for dinner. I made a house-slave joke in my head, laughing to myself. He asked what was funny, and I didn't want to answer, because I didn't want him to think that all my thoughts were about race. Though I'm probably thinking about it right now. And now. I'd been working on not censoring myself, so I told him the joke and he looked at me the way someone looks at someone else who always makes things about race.

The first guy I ever slept with was a white guy. He said he had to wash his pillows after because my hair stunk. Said it smelled burned, like kindling.

Once, a white girl I dated said she wanted me to stop pressing my hair. She said I should feel comfortable to wear it natural in front of her. That she preferred my coils. We were in a club. It was loud and obnoxious. She was yelling in my ear, "Stop burning your hair. Stop burning your hair! I can smell the heat."

Once, I felt comfortable enough with a white guy to let him watch me wrap my hair at night. I didn't grow up doing it. My mom didn't do it, and never showed me how to take care of my hair. She worked night shifts, and I often put myself to bed. I think my aunt showed me once with almond oil, but I couldn't recreate it on my own. It wasn't until I went to an HBCU, to Tennessee State University, and attended a sleepover party for the National Association of Colored Women's Clubs that I learned. All the gorgeous Black girls lined up in front of the mirrors in the large women's bathroom and wrapped their glossy, Black hair with wide brushes in long swooping motions—so much like the movement of a potter at a wheel, twirling and holding their heads on a tilted axis at strategic points until the hair was pinned in place, then wrapping it with a silk bonnet or scarf to mold and seal the shape overnight. I stared at them, trying to absorb the maneuvers for my own scalp. I stared at them the way the white guy stared at me, except his gaze was different, as if I were inside a *National Geographic.*

After George Floyd's murder, the country was on fire and I was fucking this other white guy. It was a weird and dissonant time. So many white people were reaching out to me, "checking in" and sending apologies. White people sent me money and gifts. White people sent me long poems. White people told me long stories about the Black people in their lives. White people asked me to send them poems about Black pain. In bed, I asked the white guy what he was wrestling with racially. I fell asleep as he answered, and when I woke up, he was still talking. I confessed that I'd missed a large chunk of his response. I mentioned this was a weary time for Black people and joked that he should give me a pass. I laughed. I can't remember if he did, too.

I once broke up with a white guy because he didn't want to vote for Obama.

In kindergarten, I liked this white boy. I think his name was Dan. For my fifth birthday party, my mom rented out a room at the Enchanted Forest, a kids' event venue in Los Angeles. I got to pick which story I wanted to perform for my celebration. I decided on *Sleeping Beauty* because I wanted Dan to be the prince, and I would be Princess Aurora, so he could kiss me. I remember lying on my back in a dusty costume, my hands crisscrossed over my chest with a fake rose stuck in my little grip. Ten minutes into the play, I remember thinking this was a sucky role choice, because I didn't get to participate. The distressed damsel was comatose for much of the production. I remember waiting and waiting, pinching the plastic stem tighter in my hand. But when it was time for the prince to break the spell and wake Aurora up with a juicy one, Dan recoiled in stereotypical disgust. The employees and parents were trying to coax him to kiss me, but he refused. *What about the cheek?* He refused again.

My first real kiss would be in sixth grade, with another white boy who everyone called Lil' Chris. We were in the computer lab and supposed to be practicing typing without looking at the letters. I liked Chris. He wore wide-cut JNCOs that were frayed at the hem, oversize shirts, and a wallet chain. He leaned over and opened his mouth. I obeyed. I remember his tongue felt like a dolphin dipping in and out of the ocean between our jaws. When we unfastened our preteen mouths, my braces cut his bottom lip, spilling a little droplet, a blossom of bright blood. I was embarrassed that I'd hurt him.

Once, I played Lady Anne in my high school's production of *Richard III*. In act 1, scene 2, Anne is mourning the murders of her

husband, Edward, Prince of Wales, and her father-in-law, King
Henry VI. She's crying in front of the king's coffin when Richard
III enters. She curses him, believing he's killed both men, but
somehow through his smooth and convincing repartee, Richard
seduces Anne into marrying him. He blames her beauty for his
crime. He makes her culpable. As a ploy, he even hands her his
own sword, beseeching her to execute him, saying that he doesn't
want to live in a world where Lady Anne doesn't love him. "Though
I wish thy death, / I will not be thy executioner," she says. Instead
of killing him, she takes his ring. I remember not fully understanding the complicated nuances of this conversation, but I do
now. It was about survival.

Richard III was played by a white guy named Justin whom I had
to kiss late in the scene. The thick stage makeup was dripping
from our faces in oily beads. No tongue, just lots of lip and spit. I
counted *one, two, three* in my head.

Once—years later—a white guy I dated had a hairy back that he let
me wax. I truly enjoyed ripping off the sticky strips of white paper,
loved gazing at the torn brown hair I'd yanked from the root, all
splayed and stuck to the sheets like miniature Keith Haring stick
figures. I liked making him feel a tiny jolt of pain with each violent pull.

Once, I dated a Pentecostal white guy. He said it was crucial that
I was baptized again with only the name of Jesus. Not the trinity,

or I wouldn't get into heaven. He performed my second baptism, pushing me under the water, and then a few days later we fucked in a shitty motel room near the interstate. I don't remember much of that night except the dark whir of the pulsing cars. I wasn't in my body. I wasn't in my body for most of my twenties, especially during those rare moments of near intimacy. According to my own church's doctrine, I didn't even have a body.

I often ask white guys I'm dating if I'm their first Black girl. I get a range of responses, but most often *yes*. I don't like being the first, but I don't want to be on a list consisting of only Black women, either.

I'm trying to ask better questions of myself. I'm trying to ask better questions about what I desire.

In middle school, I was dissected by two boys who seem featureless now. I can hear their voices, like the catchy chorus of an unnameable song that lingers. I remember what they said. How they bifurcated my body into white and Black features: *Her nose is Black. Her butt is white. Her lips are Black. She talks white . . .*

W. E. B. Du Bois wrote about the singular moment as a kid when he knew he was Black: "Then it dawned upon me with a certain suddenness that I was different from the others; or like, mayhap, in heart and life and longing, but shut out from their world by a vast veil. I had thereafter no desire to tear down that veil, to creep through; I held all beyond it in common contempt, and lived above it in a region of blue sky and great wandering shadows." I want to rip that veil, the thin fabric separating my binary blood—and if I can't tear it down, then I want to linger in Du Bois's *blue sky* above it, like a type of heaven for Black kids. I am still lifting my shirt to reveal not my chest but my "female horse heart," as Ada Limón wrote, claiming it as my "huge beating genius machine." I want to be seen in all my suddenness.

I was on the floor, drunk at some high school party, spinning and giggling. Lil' Chris kneeled down and put his face within an inch of mine. He pointed to the scar on his lip—a little white, plump zigzag—the wound I had so neatly carved into him. He told me he called it his *love nick*.

I did want to know the white guy's answer to my question of what he was wrestling with racially after George Floyd's brutal murder, so I asked him again when we weren't in bed. He said there was a time in his early twenties that whenever he read or heard the n-word it would get stuck in his brain on a bad loop, and he would repeat it in his mind like a caustic chant whenever he saw a Black person. I didn't know if this made me feel safe or afraid of him, or worse, both: in that liminal space between danger and desire. I think I wanted to poke that tension the most, the overlapping bubbles in the Venn diagram that named what I was afraid to reveal about myself and what turned me on. I think it aroused me to know something vulgar about him. Or maybe it was the titillating nature of confession. The false sense of intimacy it gave me. A shame that made me feel closer to him.

In college, a friend called to tell me Lil' Chris had been arrested for kidnapping and torturing a Black woman. A Black woman he thought had stolen drug money from between the lips of his mattress and box frame. He used a bat and a broken beer bottle, and I won't say what he did next. I stared at his white face framed inside the mug shot on the news. The TV screen had never seemed so bright and fuzzy until then, as if I were glimpsing a brief solar eclipse, trying to catch the moment the moon's shadow eats the sun: the taste of his tongue in my mouth.

Once, a white guy I dated said that Black pussy tastes different. Once a white guy I dated said I was *pretty for a Black girl*. Once my therapist asked why I dated so many white guys, asked if it was about power or my dad or both. Maybe I'm searching for my father in the faces of men who might look like him. A mythic composite of white avatars. Is that okay to confess? Don't we all try to scratch that first need with another, newer need?

Once, I tasted myself to see, licked my own authority from the pad of my index finger: such slow electric honey, such Black resistant joy, such thunderous manna, such historical sway, such a feverish wonder, such gorgeous cream, such a jolt of pink and brown light. Such a hard desire to be heard and seen and believed, of which I gave myself to me.

Sober with a Big O
Tawny Lara

It took more than a decade to finally discover
and embrace what turns me on.

"What turns you on?" my lover—whoever they happened to be at
the time—would ask.

"I don't know," I'd reply, then quickly deflect: "What turns
you on?"

I wasn't playing coy; I had no clue. I knew what was "supposed"
to do it for me: nipple biting, rough hands, and a wet tongue. At
least that's what porn told me I should like. That, and my body's
ability to give itself to anyone in exchange for the smallest amount
of attention.

It's not that I didn't want sex—I loved sex. The problem was that
I expected it to be like the shitty straight cliché where the woman
is game for anything as long it pleases a man. And so, I performed
the role of Woman Receiving Pleasure, more concerned with men
believing they pleased me than actually asking for what I wanted.

In fact, my sex life from fifteen until I was nearly thirty was
largely performative. Taking internet porn at cum-on-face value,
I deduced that sex was when a woman theatrically gets a man off—
nothing more. That as a woman, I was expected to dress, talk, and

fuck in ways that turned *him* on. That I should have been enthused when he wanted to finish on my face. That sex ended whenever he climaxed (no matter how quickly that was), and that foreplay was nothing more than extra credit.

Shockingly, the expectation that a penis—by simply entering me—could make me instantaneously come didn't meet reality. So I faked. And faked. I faked until it became a routine part of any sexual experience involving someone else. Whether in the context of hookups, threesomes, or long-term relationships, I reprised my performance of Woman Who Climaxes.

It took more than a decade to finally discover and embrace what turns me on. Part of what made that journey so arduous was also spending that era in denial about my substance abuse. Only years of sobriety and therapy would finally bring to light just how entwined alcohol and an unhealthy relationship with sex had become for me.

The mental health community uses the term "arrested development" for a state of suspended maturity, in which people remain at the emotional age when they first experienced trauma or turned to self-medication as a coping skill.

My emotional growth was stunted at fourteen, when an event occurred that I refer to only as the Incident. Like many people who experience trauma, I think of this moment as the line dividing my Before from my After.

Before the Incident, I was so invested in school and extra-curriculars that my mom called me Lisa Simpson. I cohosted the on-camera morning announcements and contributed to my local newspaper's teen section (my op-eds advocated for gay marriage, body positivity, and the legalization of marijuana). I loved putting a story together, even if it was just about the lunch menu or Friday night's football game.

In short, before the Incident, I was thriving.

After the Incident, my happiness was replaced with a mix of clinical depression, anxiety, and proper teen angst. Mom put me in therapy. I gave it a shot, but unpacking trauma and talking about my feelings didn't provide the instant gratification I so desperately craved. Therapy required being present for my harsh new reality, while I soon learned that I preferred escapism. I started and dropped several different SSRIs, thinking I hated them all, but the truth is I didn't stay on any long enough to see the benefits.

In my adolescent mind, I'd tried everything available to me to feel better.

The first time I got drunk and high was at a high school house party supervised by "cool" parents who didn't mind an underage rager. Everyone sang along to "Rocky Mountain Way" by the James Gang, their voices bouncing around the room, their lightness—in contrast to the heaviness I carried—drawing me in. Someone offered me a hit.

The joint touched my lips. I inhaled, held it, then exhaled, trying my hardest to emulate others so they wouldn't know it was my first time. For a second, everything went dark.

As soon as the high sank in, I couldn't stop laughing. The Incident faded from my mind. All that mattered was that moment, that music, and those people. When the joint came back around, I took a few more hits, the weight of my depression seemingly evaporating with the smoke.

When someone handed me a Smirnoff Ice, I thought, *I just smoked weed for the first time; why not try drinking while I'm at it?* One sip turned into several, which turned into finishing a few bottles.

Finally, I found relief. All it took was the numbness of instant gratification. An itch that only self-destruction could scratch.

It was the first time I remember feeling free.

In *Sex and the Single Girl*, Helen Gurley Brown describes "the Girl" as a married man's real-life fantasy and respite from married life. Sex isn't necessarily involved (though it's certainly condoned); she's essentially a young woman he shops for and adores. Helen even claims that marriages benefit from having the Girl in the picture: a husband can sate his appetite for other women without engaging in physical infidelity. Playing this role, HGB maintains, is also a coup for the Girl in question, as she gets showered with gifts and compliments.

In short, the Girl's self-esteem comes from a man's attention.

My version of the Girl was somewhere between a work wife and a woman stuck in a revolving door of delusional relationships. Drunk or high most of the time, a fourteen-year-old in the body of a grown woman, I participated in flings and long-term relationships that usually shared alcohol as the common thread. My brief list of standards was easy to satisfy: must love whiskey and rock and roll. The people (usually men, but not always) who met these requirements were either coworkers or regulars at whichever bar I was tending at the time. Each entanglement began with casual flirting while throwing back shots, followed by partying until three in the morning. If whiskey was the refined version of my first Smirnoff, then attention was the grown-up version of the bliss of that first joint.

Occasionally, these hookups turned into long-term relationships. Other times they morphed into ambiguous messes. I convinced myself I was fine with the latter; who was I to deserve more?

And this setup—a shared affinity for loud music while getting fucked up—followed me for over a decade, until I stopped drinking at twenty-nine. Sobriety plugged me into the truth I'd tried so hard to ignore: alcohol hindered my ability to distinguish reality from my version of it. My booze-soaked brain created projections of limerence, a term I learned in recovery that describes delusional, unrequited love. *He loves me; he just doesn't know it yet. I can change him. It's okay that he's sleeping with her tonight; he'll call me tomorrow.* I found comfort in these vague, unlabeled situations, tying myself to people who didn't need the clarity that I craved.

I'm not sure that I ever would've examined the unhealthy relationship dynamics of my twenties had I not taken a step back to explore my dependence on alcohol. Many of these past hookups, it's obvious now, wouldn't have happened had I been sober.

Even so, my issues were more layered than that. I drank heavily, sure, but I did so to create my own version of reality when I couldn't handle the real thing. While alcohol fueled these unhealthy relationships, my love of self-destruction—another trusted coping mechanism—kept the fire going.

At three years sober, during the last days of a heady summer, I was on my way to a Lola Kirke concert in Williamsburg, not too far from a pseudo-partner's apartment. I texted them, asking if they wanted me to come over after the show. I remember, clear as anything, reading their response: "Things recently got serious with someone else." My excitement turned to a visceral mix of nausea and despair. Just a week prior, we'd discussed going on actual dates outside of our apartments, maybe even taking a vacation together. I was optimistic that perhaps we were finally on the same page, both wanting to make it work.

In the back of an Uber, I thought only *This is when I should cry*, but my go-to feeling was anger. I went to the concert with my friend, determined to hook up with a stranger.

Enter Jack—isn't there always a Jack?—a drunk finance bro who I later found out was also on blow. He wore typical I-came-to-the-bar-from-the-office slacks and an unbuttoned, untucked shirt. He asked me generic questions, loving the sound of his own answers when I asked him more interesting questions in return. I didn't care. My pulse was racing, knowing that I was about to numb myself with attention. He was arrogant and self-righteous and talked down to me. He was *perfect*.

Jack warned me that his apartment was messy; I envisioned a few misplaced items randomly scattered around. Instead, I walked into a one-bedroom that clearly no one gave a shit about. There were clothes, books, and an unreal amount of paper strewn all over the place. A square foot of his floor served as a catchall for the pieces of his buckling ceiling.

He threw me onto the bed and we both undressed with a speed that only heightened my high. He ripped a dusty, floor-length mirror from his wall, propping it up beside me. He was drunk—no-inhibitions drunk—as he watched himself fuck me.

For the first time since I'd gotten sober, I faked an orgasm.

Unwilling to risk the subway so late in an unfamiliar neighborhood, I stayed at Jack's for as long as I could tolerate, crying silently into his pillow while my attention high morphed into a feeling of shame. The idea of escaping reality had felt more potent than my sobriety mantras—only instead of whiskey, I'd turned to sex.

When he got up to pee, I grabbed his wallet and found his ID. Seeing his personal details—name, birthday, organ-donor status—somehow made him more human than when he was inside of me, and I immediately lost interest. It reminded me of the *Sex and the City* episode when Carrie Bradshaw dates a man she meets in her therapist's waiting room. Once they sleep together, they both reveal why they're seeking help in the first place: he gets bored with women after having sex with them, and she picks the wrong men.

For an entire week after my encounter with Jack, I barely left my apartment. The days were a blur. I cried and wrote, cried and wrote. My magnum opus was titled *Fucking Men*; I filled it with all my feelings and bitter poetry, the love letters I'd never had the courage to share with almost-partners. I somehow managed to maintain my phone sessions with my therapist, who reminded me that the pain was temporary.

One afternoon, a cool breeze through my window reminded me that fall was coming. Maybe the changing season made me feel ready for a change as well; maybe I'd just cried myself out. Three years sober but tired of doing it alone, I opened my laptop and found an AA meeting in my neighborhood.

In the early days of my sobriety, I felt seen by memoirs like *Getting Off* by Erica Garza and *My Fair Junkie* by Amy Dresner. Reading about other women's various addictions made me feel empowered in my recovery instead of ashamed. Films like *Thank You for Sharing* and shows like Netflix's *Love*—both of which depict the complicated reality of living with substance abuse disorder while struggling with sex and love addiction—helped me discover that my own sexual holdups were more nuanced than the tired trope of sex addiction equating to binge drinking and compulsively fucking strangers. I realized that, like those imperfect but deserving characters, I also used physical intimacy as a resource for validation.

As I write this, I'm six years sober, and still spending my weekly therapy sessions unlearning the self-defeating lessons of my psyche. But I do know that I'm worthy of love, respect, and pleasure; I don't need to settle for someone else's bare minimum in order to feel seen. I've found my way back to my inner Lisa Simpson, eager to catch up on all the learning I missed while blacked out. I'm finally staying on antidepressants long enough for them to help.

I'm sure Helen Gurley Brown's "Girl"—the one she imagined, at least—would find satisfaction in even the shallowest attention from men. She'd be satisfied with any crumbs thrown her way.

I spent so much energy chasing those crumbs—confusing hunger with satiety, drunkenness with clarity—when the attention I craved all along was my own. Sobriety provided the gift of finally meeting, and validating, *me*. It also gave me the space to relearn my wants and desires.

"What turns you on?" my partner asks now.

"Let me show you," I say—because this time, I know.

Second Coming
Kate Crawford

As Mom used to say, "If not now, when?"
And she had an affair at eighty-five.

In real life, improbable bliss is, well, improbable. It's 2012, and I'm sixty-five, four foot eleven, and on the flabby side of stout. My clothes are beyond their sell-by date. And I'm exhausted from assisting my ninety-two-year-old mother in her slide to the other side.

Twelve hours ago, I left my mother's closed-up house in Montana, where I'd worn my big-girl pants all week. The first tears arrived as I snapped shut the plane's seat belt, then I cried nonstop to San Francisco. With any luck, I comforted myself, I'd be back in my Sebastopol cocoon before dark.

Back on the ground, I realize: solace will come only as I wrap new life around my grief. But how? As the airport shuttle travels through Marin, we pass the turnoff for Nick's Cove, a favorite restaurant. *Ahh, oysters. A good choice.* In Montana, I'd met—and fancied—a man who would be visiting next month and had asked me to have dinner. Momentarily, my mind turns from the dismal to the delightful—a real relief. I possess a low tolerance for being swamped by my emotions.

Over the line in Sonoma County, California's golden hour silhouettes the grapevines flinging up their trellises. I need my own fling. At my sixtieth birthday party, I'd told my family, "Watch out—I plan to have a sexy sixties." That plan died as Mom did.

After picking up my car, I head for Andy's, a fruit stand that also conveniently sells ice cream, and then down a pint of Cherry Garcia in the solitude of my back porch. The birds quiet, the crickets rev up, and the gloaming fades. I stumble to bed and grab the first book in reach: David Brooks's *The Social Animal*.

Brooks begins by following the dating rituals of a heterosexual couple. They lean forward in their chairs, glance sideways at each other, and lick their lips. I lean forward in bed, glance sideways out of my glasses, and lick my lips.

Next, the woman in the book does a head cant, exposing her neck and signaling arousal. I cant my head and expose my neck above my PJs.

Enough. I snap the book shut and pitch it across the room.

I want nothing more than to lay across a big brass bed again. In the 1960s, I'd romped through my first coming-of-age. My passion? Social justice with a capital J. My pastime? Sex with a capital S.

The sex part started in college. I would date and mate and then hang free, though never alone—I had remarkable friends. Many graduates planned a trip down the aisle; I planned a trip to Kenya. I wasn't opposed to marriage and kids, but I was afraid of becoming a kept woman in the form of a suburban housewife. I wanted to live my own life, make my own decisions, and have sex. And so I did. Until I didn't.

Where's the jazz now? The waves, the moonlight. Teases, canoodles, and footsie under the table. French kisses and big smackeroos. Beguiled, enthralled, disrobing. Tickles, nibbles, suckles. Trembling flesh laid bare. Curled toes and tangled legs. Whispers amped from moaning groans to high-pitched yelps. Ricochets between painful pleasure and pleasurable pain. Explore, suck, kiss, slap. Frenzied gyrations. Unstoppable convergence. Hurtle to primal scream.

Improbable bliss.

That's it, I decide. I'm resuscitating my sexy sixties campaign.

The next morning, I start the hunt for seductive intimates. When I was younger, I scoured Filene's Basement for real lingerie. My favorite find was a pair of French-cut bikinis like the ones Barbra Streisand wore in *The Owl and the Pussycat*. I doubt that anyone who saw them on me either made the connection or cared about it, but I did. They made me feel sexy. Ergo, I expect that replacing my worn-out, stretched-out, and soon-to-be-thrown-out knickers with alluring, black-lace versions will help restore those sexy vibes. I rule out peek-a-boo and crotchless numbers, learn how to measure myself from an online video, ogle for a while longer, then order two matching sets.

Next, I'm off to my local library. I need a sexpert to best Brooks—or at least a newer edition of *Our Bodies, Ourselves*. When I first read it in 1976, I uncovered the amazing information that I had a clitoris. Neither Mom, the Kotex pamphlet, nor my high school health teacher had mentioned such a thing. Perhaps they didn't know either.

Sonoma County's reference system unveils a mind-blowing 3,938 books about sex, including an entire section on senior sex.

Unhappily, the books authored by wise, older women are all at other branches, but when I hit my twenty-book reserve limit, I scoop up the younger sexperts from the shelves to take with me.

Abashed, I drift to the front desk. I know the librarian. I know he knows these are not my typical reads. With a straight but reddening face he checks me—and my books—out.

Back home and fortified with coffee, I skim the thirty- and fortysomething authors. Their audience seems to be teens and naive middle-aged divorcées. Their authorial view cops to neither passion nor pleasure, the tone alternating between dust-bowl dry and fear-mongering—though the thing that scares the bejeezus out of me now is STIs, not pregnancy, which seems to be the only difference between these manuals and my high school health class. This advice is decidedly not sexy. Nonetheless, condoms are still the answer. I make a note on my mental to-do list to buy some.

The last thing I need is an STI. I already have a long-haul case of myalgic encephalitis/chronic fatigue syndrome, which sometimes results in an 80 percent loss of activity, with fierce on-again, off-again pain. At forty-six, I'd sold my perpetually understaffed, twenty-two-room New Hampshire inn and restaurant that I'd run alone and settled down in the Sebastopol house. My doctor had prescribed "aggressive rest." In the beginning, I was asleep or lying down for at least twenty hours a day. No time, no energy, for sex.

Now, the loss of my mom has opened up my dance card. That, and after twenty-two years of resting aggressively, I can manage with only fourteen to sixteen hours of repose a day.

The first black-lace items arrive with the mail. Lacking a full-length mirror, I stand on the toilet to scrutinize my finds. My cleavage hangs in a cloud, the part of the bathroom vanity I can't reach to dust. The initial tries are easy nos. I spurn panties, no matter how gorgeous, that yield a four-hipped look. Same goes for bras that overflow (unflatteringly) with an embarrassment of riches.

Enter the retro numbers: high-waisted panties with a V-indent pointing south and a satin push-up bra that counters years of gravity's pull. I peer into the mirror. For the first time in my life, I don't lift my shoulders in a that-will-have-to-do shrug. *We've come a long way together*, I silently say to my body. I throw up an arm and swing out a hip. *You've suffered for sure, but now look at you, you sexy thing!*

Elated, I head back to the library for the crone tomes I've requested from other branches. They portray senior lovemaking as different, yes, but as provocative as the sex of our lithesome twenties. Better yet, they include a road map to an erogenous path: buff up the pelvic floor muscles, score some lube, and then—self-pleasure.

My old vibrator is as timeworn as I am. Four decades ago, I scuffed into San Francisco's Good Vibrations and bought the first toy the groovy shop attendant recommended: a dull plastic wand that's since yellowed with age. A truncheonish rod topped with a hard ball, it had two speeds: *Is someone knocking?* and *Slam-bang thank you, ma'am.*

In my younger years, I played Crosby, Stills & Nash, drank red wine, and took my time. But lately, the wand is more of an insomnia-fighting tool. Together we can scarcely pull off a quickie a month.

Time for a change.

My computer reveals a carnival of vibrator varieties. Alongside the tried-and-true wands are more lifelike options, some with a potent-looking clit finger. Others lean toward novelty, shaped like bunnies and rubber duckies. Since I was last in the market, someone's invented vibrators that operate remotely. I check the reviews to confirm that yep, people do each other in public—yet another tech advance that escapes me.

I fancy the luxurious, sensuous, and cord-free. Of course, these are a more substantial investment. But as Mom used to say, "If not now, when?" And she had an affair at eighty-five.

Ultimately, I embrace a handsome, crescent-moon-shaped beau with a swelling golden handle. Eight speeds, eight tempos, soft to the touch, and—*ooh la la*—waterproof. Seductive black is out of stock, so I order sultry aqua blue.

While waiting for it to arrive, I return to the sexperts to gather advice on moving from self-bliss to bliss with a flesh-and-blood man. Kindness, mutual attraction, and laughter are my must-haves. In the reordered world of senior sex, nice guys finish first. Looks, status, and college degrees don't even make the list.

I do everything the sexy elders suggest: Kegel exercises, Ben Wa balls, soft jazz, flamenco lessons. I work out with a hula hoop and flirt with every man I meet. A friend suggests I write down my fantasies; I do that, too. I draw the line, though, at taking up golf to meet men—one of my first lovers golfed. God, how it bored me. My campaign becomes an obsession, gently diffusing my grief. I launch into all the living I've yet to live.

And then, a week later, a package hits my deck. I wait ten minutes to avoid my chatty mail carrier, retrieve the box, hustle it back inside, and rip into it. The hue: intense, exotic, come-hither. I am transported. A salty breeze stirs my sarong. The sea at my feet is an exquisite turquoise. It's my new favorite color.

I name my vibrator Monsieur Turque, short for turquoise. He needs four hours to get his charge on. I plug him in next to my bed and promptly fall asleep.

Steamy and damp, I wake from my nap feeling charged myself. I flip the sheet off my naked body and glance at M. Turque. He, too, is ready.

Teething open a packet of lube, I dip in my pinky and moisten my breasts for a little breeze-tease. I trail a line around my belly button, cover my mons Venus, then squirt a glob on herself. Startled by the cold, she sneezes and dives under her petals.

I turn on M. Turque, slow and low. He circles the perimeter of my pleasure and snoops round the lotus bud. I up his tempo. Frolic. Tease. Stroke. He skis the ridges of my desire. Shudder. Tremble. Thaw. I'm lost in an erotic hothouse. M. Turque quakes before my carnal gates. Nuzzling. Fondling. Goosing. He eases in. Erotic eruption nears.

M. Turque shuts off.

My hips pitch away. Desperate fingers poke at buttons. Monsieur bursts to life again. Toes curl, rump grinds, knees contract toward chest. At last, I'm transported to the stratosphere.

If I'm Lonely
Vanessa Friedman

Most days, it feels like I won't ever be in
love again. Most days, that feels okay.

The first person I fuck after I break up with my ex-girlfriend is, unfortunately, my ex-girlfriend. I've never had sex with an ex before because I'm like, good at boundaries or whatever—but I was never good at boundaries with her.

It happens after our last couples therapy session, the one we went to even though we'd already broken up because we'd scheduled it and she wanted to keep the appointment and I felt guilty so we did. I wanted a clean break—no calls, no texts, no contact, at least for a few weeks, maybe months—but she wanted the opposite.

You should try to compromise, our therapist said.

At first, postbreakup sex is some of the best we ever have. She's mean in a way she never would be when we were together. She straps on gets on top fucks me hard and I like it she calls me a slut and I like it she slaps my tits and I like it she hurts me and I really like it. Afterward I sleep over and we hold each other and maybe we cry—honestly I don't remember, but I do know that in the morning I feel like shit.

When I leave, I see the bleeding hearts in her front yard have bloomed. I take a picture and post it to Instagram with a short caption in an effort to cheer myself up: *Found my favorite flower, today's gonna be a good one.*

She comments later: *Sure, it's the flowers that make today good*, with a winky-face emoji. This feels like it could become a habit, like we could slip right back into dating, which is the whole reason I wanted to cease contact in the first place.

You absolutely cannot sleep with her again, Lisa says when I confess. I'm too embarrassed to tell anyone besides my best friend.

I know, I say.

No seriously, she persists. *You are holding her entire heart in your hand and it is so unfair to lead her on or give her false hope.*

I nod; she's right, I know.

After we're done—done with compromises, done for good—it feels like I will never have sex with anyone who isn't my ex-girlfriend ever again. I feel ugly sad undesirable broken.

I guess I'm just done having sex, I say to Lisa, and she rolls her eyes at me but I mean it. That is how it feels.

River works at the queer-women-owned sex toy shop in my neighborhood. They're in their thirties and poly and kinky and sadistic and so hot I cannot quite believe they want to go on a date with me. I don't know much about them, just know their Mars is in Scorpio and that means they could tease me forever and be satisfied just know they have the word CHUBBY tattooed across their belly in all caps just know that we're both so busy we make a date for the end of May at the end of April but then we can't wait or maybe I can't wait I've got that Mars in Aries you know but anyway I find myself on their doorstep at midnight on a Sunday even though I've got deadlines and travel plans and work in the morning because they texted *why don't you just come over right now / what's stopping you / no really what's stopping you*.

We don't fuck this time—it turns out they're sincere when they say they could tease me forever—but we kiss, a lot, and they leave bruises on my tits. They are surprised I said yes when they asked me to come over in the middle of the night but I'm not. I've been saying no to myself for a really long time. I'm done with that now. Now I only have *yes, please, thank you*. Now I have a new story.

I've been to A-Camp—an annual gathering of four hundred queer babes in Southern California—many times before, but in the past I was always partnered. I spent my twenties in serial monogamous relationships; now I'm almost thirty and I'm finally solo.

On the last night of camp, there is a dance and we're all teenagers again; so much of being queer is reliving milestones, trying to get it slightly more right than we did in our youth. I have a crush on everyone, but I have a particular crush on Noah; she's Jewish and wants to be a rabbi, she's obnoxious and butch, she's in her early twenties but her dark hair is already peppered with silver strands and she keeps it long on one side, buzzed short on the other. I tell her in passing *I like when butch babes pull my hair I like when they do it and tell me I'm pretty* and I think Jesus Christ Vanessa do we ever leave that childhood playground do we ever unlearn the problematic ways our mothers told us boys were flirting when they hurt us but I also think—who cares. I *do* like it when butch babes pull my hair. Maybe it's the patriarchy or maybe it just feels good.

At the dance I make out with Finn I make out with Al I make out with Molly I make out with Rose I make out with Jessie I almost

make out with Lou but Summer asks me not to and I'm annoyed
but I listen because I love her and whatever.

Your breakup tour is inspirational, Rose says in my ear and her
burnt-red lipstick is still on my mouth and I love her and I wonder
why I spent my twenties partnered I wonder how much sex I will
have in the future I wonder why it took me so long to get here I
wonder what was stopping me.

Near the end of the night, I'm dancing onstage surrounded by
friends, my velvet snakeskin dress drenched in sweat and someone else's tequila when Noah comes up behind me and pushes her
body against mine. My ass meets her hips and her hand is in my
hair. She tugs, not gently, and puts her mouth near my neck.

Let's leave, she says, and we do.

My body is still bruised from River's impact the week before,
Noah's mouth tastes like she's been fucking someone else, we do
not belong to each other, I love it. My desire lives like an object
in my throat, like glitter on my skin. We get back to my room and
we're alone my dress comes off she pushes me down she straddles
me she pulls my hair I'm wet I want her I want everything.

She unbuttons her shirt but leaves it on, leaves her sports bra
in place, leaves her pants zipped and buttoned, finally takes off
her boots and ties up her hair but that's all. I'm naked on the bed
now, on my knees, she asks if I want her to spank me and I say *yes*
I beg I say *please* I am so good she tells me so I know it I say *thank
you*. She hits me again and again, her palm on my ass, and I say
more, more, more, I say *please*, my brain unlocks and I don't have
a single thought just the bright hot pain on my ass that spreads
through my cunt into my stomach, *please don't stop* I say and she
laughs, *you're very good at this* she says she puts two fingers inside
me then three then four I beg *more* roll my body over her fingers

still inside me take a deep breath push down open wide she looks up at me *holy shit you're so hot* I grin it feels so good *I can take more* we go slow soon her whole fist in my cunt soon her eyes wide I love the way a butch looks when her hand disappears inside me for the first time her whole face open reverent blessed thankful.

She fucks me hard for a long time, fucks me until we both need to stop to drink some water.

Do you *need anything*, I ask, my body between her legs, my head resting on her bare stomach.

She says no, says she's satisfied.

Then she plays with my hair while telling me about misogyny in the Old Testament, teasing me about wanting to take home a nice Jewish boy.

A few hours before breakfast she says, *I should go*, and she does.

I text Lisa *okay good news I had sex again no one panic* then I fall asleep.

When I wake up three hours later, Lisa has texted me back: three emoji faces, all rolling their eyes, and then, *duh, literally no one was worried except you*.

If River helped me locate my desire, Noah helped me locate my desirability.

I get home from camp and embark on a slutty summer. I tell all my friends, I name it, I want it known: *I am having a Slutty Summer.*

I fuck River for the first time, then Travis, then Parker, then Casey when she visits. I meet Tay, Lisa's new roommate, and flirt so hard she tells me *I think your oven is permanently set to four hun-*

dred. I laugh; we end up in her bedroom making out against her closed door. I go out dancing and make out with strangers who stay mostly strangers. I go to Jac's good-bye party and make out with Dawn.

How did you find someone to make out with at a goodbye party where we know and dislike almost everyone? Summer asks me, only half-joking.

Aggressive cleavage and a can-do attitude go a long way, I say, and we laugh and laugh and laugh.

I feel like one of those characters in the weird genre of makeover movies from the nineties, the shy nerdy girls who take off their glasses and put on a prom dress and suddenly the most popular football player notices them. Except I'm still wearing my glasses and I put on a velvet crop top and purple lipstick and a fake septum piercing—but it's true that suddenly everyone notices me. Or maybe I notice everyone for the first time.

This is so fun to experience, Lexi says one night when I get drunk and make out with her, then her partner. *You've always been such a flirt and now you can finally act on it!*

Near the end of the summer, my friends and I all buy tickets to see Janelle Monáe. There's rain in the forecast and the show is outside but somehow the weather holds off and we're treated to a perfect sunset, a real fucking treat in Portland.

God loves queer people, I yell at the sky, explaining the weather, explaining the universe.

Every single queer in Portland is at the concert—my ex is here, River is here, River's date is here, some of my other dates are here.

I don't know exactly how to act around all of them so I focus on flirting with everyone else. Finn teases me about it and Clara, his girlfriend, joins in.

She's just having a nice time, Clara says, borrowing the language I've been using to describe my summer. I'm moving to the East Coast soon for school and I'm convinced no one there will want to fuck me because New Yorkers hate fat people, so it's important to make the most of Portland. We all laugh, even River and their date, and I'm pleased.

I am, I say. *I am having a very nice time!*

On one of my last nights in the Pacific Northwest I have dinner with Bobby and Tess, my Land Dyke elders. I've driven four hours south to their rural homestead to say goodbye to them; they're my family. They've been together for more than a decade and they've each got twenty years on me; their perspectives matter a lot. They knew me before I moved to Portland, before I met my ex. They knew me when I landed in Oregon five years ago, grieving a different ex and a community fallout and a friend breakup that cracked my heart neatly in half. I lived with them for a year after that, trying to heal. They've seen me lonely, really lonely, in a way I haven't felt in years, didn't even feel after my most recent breakup.

After dinner, we all hug good night, and before I retire to my tent under the old Madrone trees and they climb the hill up to their dreamy cob house, Tess gives me an extra squeeze. I've told her and Bobby about everything—how badly my ex is taking our breakup, how happy I am in spite of it, how nervous I am for school in the fall, how this summer I'm having such a nice time. *I am so excited for you, babe*, Tess says. *You have so much life ahead of you. You have so much good sex ahead of you!*

Sometimes there's no metaphor. Sometimes you're just having so much good sex.

I've been single for six months and living in New York for six weeks the night June reads me "Song." She's a new friend from school and I invite her to my apartment one night to drink wine and do homework. She sees Adrienne Rich's *The Fact of a Doorframe* on my bookshelf and says, *My favorite poem lives in this book!* We're tipsy and I'm trying not to kiss her.

She sits on the floor so I sit on the sofa and she opens the book to page 104—I've since bookmarked it—and begins: *You're wondering if I'm lonely.* I do not take my eyes off June; my brain clicks into the rhythm of Adrienne's words; I feel alive I feel alone I feel lonely it is good.

I hold my breath for the duration of the poem and when it's over I keep staring at June and she looks up at me and neither of us moves for a long time until finally she says, *I should probably go home.*

We'll kiss in a bar in Brooklyn six months later. I'll tug on her tie she'll tug on my hair I'll giggle so will she.

When are you going to fuck me, I'll ask, teasing but serious, and she'll smile but close up a little bit, too.

I'm still in love with Mary, she'll say, referencing her shitty ex, and I'll nod and shrug like, no big deal, whenever you're ready, babe, I'm not going anywhere.

And it's true. I'll be right here when June wants to fuck me. I'm not in love with anyone, not like that, haven't been for a year, maybe longer if I'm being truthful.

Most days, it feels like I won't ever be in love again. Most days, that feels okay.

A few days after June reads me the Adrienne Rich poem, I'm sitting on the toilet scrolling through Instagram when it hits—such profound loneliness I'm worried I might pass out.

It's autumn and the leaves are changing colors on the suburban New York trees and soon it will get cold, really cold, and I'll have to buy a new coat. I've been single for half a year. I rent a studio and live alone for the first time in my life. I have a queen-size bed all to myself. I am pooping with the door open, a real fucking luxury after living in community since I moved out of my parents' house.

I don't remember what photo made me feel so alone. Maybe I've forgotten on purpose in an effort to avoid ever conjuring that emotion back into my chest. Was it an engagement announcement of a couple I actually believe might make it, as rare as they may be? A particularly cute adopted pet? The kind of gushing caption that I used to write about my ex, in the beginning, when the big feelings took over and I really felt like I was falling in love?

What if we're too old to ever fall in love like that again, I text Rose. *What if we all have too much baggage now what if we know too much about how shitty being partnered can be what if I'm so lonely I die what if I die alone what if?*

Rose and I text every day since camp. She lives alone in Minneapolis; she divorced her now ex-husband a few months before I broke up with my ex. Every day we say good morning and we say good night, we complain about work, we gossip about everyone we know, we send screenshot after screenshot after screenshot, we laugh so hard together. *I'M CACKLING* I text when she makes me laugh out loud; *lmao* she texts and I can hear her sarcastic chuckle. We talk about relationship models, about love, about realistic expectations, about sex and intimacy and partnership and situationships.

I want to marry you, I text her one day, early on, and she laughs, says she's probably never getting married again. I let it be a joke even though I was maybe serious.

We settle into deep-love best friendship instead. To a lot of people it would look like I'm in a long-distance relationship; I guess I am.

The night I think I might die of loneliness, Rose texts me until I fall asleep. *I know what you mean*, she writes calmly. *I feel that way too sometimes. It's okay. You're okay. I love you. I'm right here. You're okay, you're okay, you're okay.*

I fall asleep holding my phone. In the morning I wake up and the dull ache in my heart is gone, like magic or avoidance or some combination of the two.

How are you angel? Rose texts.

So much better, I text back. *I think I just need to get fucked soon lol.*

Almost immediately, I see the animated three dots indicating that she's writing back appear: *lmao same.*

A year after my breakup, I'm back in Portland for spring break. It's Lisa's birthday and we go to a karaoke bar to celebrate. At the bar I run into a friend I haven't seen in ages, not since before I moved. She and her girlfriend have just broken up—they were together for almost eight years—and she tells me she's heartbroken.

What do I do? she asks.

I don't know, I say, thinking she might be afraid to be alone. *The thing is, I have been really fucking lonely sometimes this past year. But even so, no matter how lonely I am, it is still always better than trying to deal with another human being! I would rather be lonely for the rest of my life than ever date someone seriously again! And anyway, even when I'm partnered, I think it's my friends that make me feel less lonely.*

She does not look soothed. She looks at me very seriously and says, *I feel like I am never going to have sex again.*

Oh! You are definitely *going to have sex again*, I tell her, thrilled to have an answer to this particular fear. I think back to last summer, remember the promise of my Land Dyke elder Tess. Now I repeat it for my newly single friend with confidence: *You have so much good sex ahead of you.*

The Greatest Pleasure
Xoài Phạm

I didn't know that everything I feared would live right
beside everything I would come to love about sex work.

"You can take off the condom," I said to him between labored
breaths.

Our rhythm paused.

"Really?" he asked.

"If you aren't having sex with anyone else, like you said,
then yes."

He was the first of them to say, "I love you." The client I'd been
seeing the longest.

When he slid back inside me, I watched his face change: head
tilted just slightly, mouth opening wider. I stared into his face, his
eyes closed, like this moment of vulnerability was a secret I was
given to keep. I was a voyeur to his deepest self; I was inside of him
as much as he was inside of me.

For the next few moments, I watched his head move just
slightly to the rhythm of our bodies, like this hotel room was an
ocean, the bed a raft. I could float with him for a short while.

At this point in my life, I was existing in the in-betweens. I was lonely.

Each day, I endured stares. People took videos on their phones. The train, the sidewalk, the grocery store, all battlegrounds. When I left my evening shift, I'd squeeze my cat-shaped keychain—disguised as a novelty item but designed to pierce skin—until I got home, sometimes as late as 2:00 a.m. My gender expression was an anomaly to the public. I was too angry to admit that I was beaten down, that I desperately wanted to exchange the glares for a gentle gaze. I wanted to be held. To lie in bed and forget what time it was.

I didn't think I'd find this relief when I started taking cash for access to my body. I didn't know that everything I feared would live right beside everything I would come to love about sex work.

When I was young, what I learned about intimacy—and by extension, sex—was that it wasn't meant for me. As children, we are groomed to obsess over romance before we've even hit puberty. We declare our crushes. Pass notes. Write each other's names in embellished penmanship. I told everyone I liked Christa when I really liked Austin. I knew I couldn't tell anyone my true feelings, though I wasn't sure why.

While most of my classmates went on to have multiple relationships throughout our school years, I was in an endless state of pining, everything always out of reach. I toed the line of intimacy only in writing. As if my fingers dancing on a keyboard was the same as grazing someone's arm.

I was eighteen when I had sex for the first time. So eager that I didn't care how dangerous it was. I did as I was told and met him at a train station, before walking back to his house in Queens. I remember him mixing me a drink. Forgetting to watch him pour it. I remember him coming up from behind to hug me, his body almost twice the size of mine.

Instructing me throughout the night, he showed me how to open my jaw while tucking my teeth away, how to relax my body before penetration. He slowly guided himself into me, knowing to go easy each time I felt a jab of pain. When we finished, I went home and never spoke to him again.

For the next few months, I swam through a rapid current of men. There was the towering Italian photographer who distracted me with *Kung Fu Panda* before he started eating me out. At a tiny park by the East River in Manhattan, I gave a blow job to a Russian medical student while people stared from their windows. There was the man who was more than twice my age, who held me in his lap as I gazed down at the twinkling Chelsea cityscape.

Sometimes I had men over at my apartment twice in the same day, between classes. Their hungry eyes were a temporary salve for the fear I had yet to recognize: the more my femininity emerged, the more poisonous my surroundings became.

I lived in two opposing worlds. In public, I walked the streets and encountered confused, uncomfortable, often hostile faces. In private, I was the object of lust. I needed proof that I was lovable, not just a plaything.

It would take several years before I admitted to myself: what men did to me behind closed doors was not love. It was a momentary escape, for the both of us.

The bitter scent of burnt hair. The small, excruciating *beep* of the pulsing laser machine.

I had graduated from college at twenty and started working at a sex retail boutique that served the ritzy Upper East Side of Manhattan. I made just enough to pay rent. There was no way I could handle a monthly four-hundred-dollar bill for laser hair removal. I knew I had to come up with the money somehow. Choosing not to proceed with it wasn't an option.

Each time the laser pricked my upper lip, the aesthetician would place her hand on my mouth to subdue the pain. I started to hold my breath involuntarily. Tears formed at the corners of my eyes. It felt like drowning.

Worse than the hour-long session to rid myself of unwanted hair was the anticipation of it. Every time I took the thirty-minute train ride to the salon, I felt ashamed of my trans body. I could only think of it as a source of pain.

My mom didn't know that I was doing sex work. She wasn't aware of how much I spent on laser treatments each month. She had no idea that I'd gone under the knife to have my Adam's apple reduced. She didn't even know I was transitioning.

Is it fair to be mad at someone for something they couldn't possibly know about? My mother, the first image of femininity I witnessed. The first model of intimacy I experienced.

I thought of the time she slapped my hand in preschool after discovering my painted nails. While the others had cleaned up after an art project, I'd sloppily scrawled all the different colors of markers across my nails. The act was subconscious, devoid of deliberation. I was emulating what I saw in feminine figures. Maybe I was just trying to become my mother.

What would she say if she knew how her child was making money?

Still, I called her every day. Told her the place I worked sold clothes instead of sex toys. Made no mention of the men I was seeing when she asked about a boyfriend.

"It's mango season," she said.

"I'm craving them," I responded.

"Every time I eat a mango, I think of you and how much you love them."

A few months later, I named myself the Vietnamese word for mango: Xoài.

My shift ended just after midnight. I'd been drinking with a co-worker that evening—we often snuck liquor into the utility closet behind the cash register, taking sips when it was slow. Afterward, I stumbled into the night toward a nearby hotel where my client's business meeting had just ended. Behind the glint of the revolving doors, I noticed he was better-looking than most of the others I had met. Tall, statuesque.

He shook my hand and we walked back to the elevators. I glanced around at the men in suits, who worked late hours like I did but made more money than my family could even fathom.

To escape the uncomfortable silence, I scrutinized the orange lights that lined the floors and ceilings of the elevator. When we reached his suite, he uncorked a bottle of wine and poured me a glass. We watched the passersby out the window, small and completely unaware that they were being observed, each with their own unique experience of the day. He talked about his two children, his house in Prague.

When we were sufficiently tipsy, I asked to use the restroom, where four hundred dollars was tucked beneath the tissue box. I cleaned myself up, changed into lingerie, and reemerged. He was sitting on the bed, waiting as if I were to make a grand appearance. His eyes had changed; he was less guarded.

"Let me give you a massage," I offered.

He disrobed and lay on his stomach. This was my usual routine. It meant I was the one with the upper hand in case things got violent. I sat on top of his buttocks and rubbed oil into his shoulders, kneading what seemed to be endless knots. His back made my hands look even smaller than they were.

At some point, he found a way to turn me over onto my back. A slight smile. His hair glowing red from the beam of light diffusing around his head. He kissed my neck, my collarbones, my nipples, my belly button. He started inserting one, then two fingers inside of me, slowly massaging.

"I want you to play with yourself," he said.

I obeyed, running my fingers along the length of my shaft, tapping the head as I started getting wet. He increased the speed of his fingers, penetrating me while he sucked on my nipples. Soon, I climaxed and came on my stomach.

The next thing I remember is waking up to his shy smile. He was lying on my stomach, watching me. Embarrassment crept over my face as I realized where I was and apologized for falling asleep. He watched me for a few more moments and then kissed me. I was still in a dream state, not quite awake. Time was silent here.

Eventually, I remembered that I had another shift in the morning and made my way home.

We all crave the reminder that we're worthy of love, but we fear being trapped in vulnerable places, afraid that we'll be forced to see ourselves as all that we are.

Some of us work through our fears better than others. Of the many men I met along the path home to myself, I was surprised at how alike we were. No matter how much our lives looked different, I knew what I saw in their eyes. We wanted the same things. What's different are the obstacles that stand between us and what we want.

The moment of intimacy when their eyes lock with mine is when they can exhale. When their desires have freedom.

Sex workers aren't killed because sex work is inherently dangerous. A culture of shame and violent policing is what makes sex work dangerous. If a client had decided to rape me or force me to do things I didn't permit, he would likely face no consequences. Because reporting it to the police would mean I would be arrested, or worse, assaulted again—by the police.

Community organizers often repeat the phrase "Sex work is work." It's true. And sex work is more than just that. Sex work can be important work. It can sometimes be sacred work. But it should never be the only available work.

Sex workers can help turn a room into an opening—toward our softest selves. Where loneliness is at least briefly sidelined. Where people, in the right circumstances, are fed something we all need: healing.

I'm not single anymore. I'm in love for the first time.

It's been about a year since I stopped taking clients.

For the past month, I've thought about discontinuing Truvada, a pill that helps prevent HIV if taken daily. It's been a battle over whether I can allow myself to trust my partner. I hear in my head the first thing my parents said to me when I told them I was queer: "Don't get AIDS."

I was afraid that the danger taunting me daily would lead to a sexual assault, and that I would contract HIV in the process, creating even more obstacles in my life. The fear was like a fresh wound each time I met someone new, each time I walked out in public alone.

Over the years, there were men who had pressured me to take off the condom. There have been others who removed it without my knowledge, claiming afterward that I had seemed to consent.

The one thing I could control was whether I took that pill each day. Now, I'm being asked to have some faith. I've been given the opportunity to soften. There's someone I trust enough not to need a condom or Truvada. And that scares me more than anything I've previously faced. It feels impossible. It feels like I'm being deceived.

I've been gifted with a moment to pause. To slow down and look around.

I had planted the seeds of safety in my life. I protected myself fiercely. I learned my boundaries. I was my own advocate. I extended compassion to others, even when I didn't have much for myself. And I built the relationships I'd needed so I could ask for help.

I began to knit together all the small moments of tenderness that I felt with each of the men I met, whether or not money was involved; finally, it felt like I was coming home. I saw myself, whole for the first time, through this sweet man's eyes. While I was trying so hard to become the kind of person that someone would love, I had along the way become the kind of person that I love.

A tremendous love. A love that kept me alive, kept me wanting more for myself. I wrapped my arms around my chest, touched the stretch marks across my back, and witnessed a love story I didn't know was there.

I was everything I needed.

Apartment
Seema Reza

> To live with other people is to be responsible for
> protecting them from your moods. Or perhaps, to
> protect the delicate gift of your moods from them.

When I was already beyond the acceptable age for make-believe,
I invented a game called Apartment. Playing house a few years
prior, I'd cooked dinner and scolded imaginary children while
waiting for my husband (played by a giant stuffed bear) to come
home. I'd talked on the phone and bustled about like I'd seen
women do. But in Apartment, I pretended I was renting my bedroom from strangers and that I lived there alone alone alone.
Nothing *happened* in Apartment. I didn't know anyone; there was
no romance.

I joined my friends in "normal" teenage chatter: boys we
liked, our weddings, outfits circled in magazines. I experimented
with a curling iron and lipstick, high heels from Payless. My re-
torts were quick, I chose dare over truth, could make anyone
laugh. But it felt exhausting, performative.

Apartment was about the absence of social exchange, freedom
from measuring myself against others through external determi-
nants of my likability, my goodness, my value. I would go outside,

stroll through our suburban neighborhood, and come back in to eat something simple before retiring to my bedroom to read.

Aside from characters in books and movies, the only adult I'd known to live all alone was my uncle Shamim. After stints in each of his brothers' basements, scandalizing their wives one by one with his alcoholism and the cruelty that rode the fumes of his whiskey breath, he moved into a condo owned by another family member. His last chance to get clean, get it together, get a wife, and grow up.

For my thirteenth birthday, my mother (prudish in all areas but literature) gave me a copy of *My Wicked, Wicked Ways*, a collection of poems by Sandra Cisneros, my favorite writer. The glossy, lipstick-red dust jacket featured a woman reclining on a green sofa, naked except for white shoes and a book draped over her chest. I read the brazen and bewildering poems and felt braver: Cisneros smoking cigarettes in Paris, refusing to wash any man's clothes, to bend to anyone, *even if she was lonely*. Her lines inspired a fierce tenderness toward my own melancholy: "I want and want my grief—each cell must have its fill—and I want more of it."

In Apartment I answered to no one, owed no one. I was invisible, and sparse. In Apartment I drank coffee and didn't bother with hot meals. In Apartment, I wasn't a girl or a woman or a man, just an adult person in jeans and sneakers. I wasn't pretty, and my teeth weren't crooked. I felt dark and brooding and weightless and relieved. Floating. At home in myself, performing for no one.

I moved into my first apartment at eighteen: a white-walled, beige-carpeted one-bedroom on the first floor of a brick high-rise. I furnished it with IKEA furniture and secondhand black leather couches. A large bookshelf lined with novels along the living room wall, a queen platform bed with a blue duvet and a blond-wood headboard. The signature arching, five-pronged spider lamp of late 1990s bachelors. No television. With my first paycheck at a legal temp agency, I bought an enormous mirror discounted at a furniture outlet due to the crack in its silver frame.

I was engaged. My fiancé was twenty-one. I'd met him a year before in Dhaka, Bangladesh, where I'd been sent to live with my grandparents for being dangerously atheist and non-Muslim and wild and uncontrollable.

Uncontrollable. They meant the word as a criticism; I wore it as a badge. My fiancé saw it as a challenge.

I knew I wouldn't really be free of my parents until I got married; he couldn't move to America unless I sponsored him. And really, I loved him.

But I loved that quiet apartment, too. I'd return from long hours spent scanning documents and printing emails for corporate mergers and prepare refrigerated tortellini or fettuccine for dinner. I'd sit in one of the narrow, loosely assembled metal dining chairs and read a novel and smoke a cigarette at the glass table afterward. It was all so luxurious.

In the complete privacy of that apartment, I had my first orgasm, lying on my back in the bathtub, angled under the rushing faucet, the door closed even though I was alone. I'd felt pleasure during sex, but I'd never reached climax. Only alone, unwatched, could I discover what I needed, the depth of what my body could feel.

When my two sisters and I were children, my mother would show us her wedding jewelry set, her mother's, my father's mother's. My mother collected other pieces of jewelry and put them away for each of her daughters, showing us before locking them in the safe: "When you get married." I didn't have the capacity to imagine a story beyond the one Bollywood and Hollywood agreed upon: that once I was pretty enough, Prince Charming in dark sunglasses would smile at me, I would smile back, and my life would begin. The door out of my father's house would open directly into my husband's.

I was on borrowed time, eating pasta and reading in silence. My fiancé's arrival loomed.

When my first niece was born, the bottom of my heart dropped out like a trapdoor, exposing a capacity for more love than I'd imagined. I'd liked babies well enough before that, but they could be annoying, and motherhood seemed like too much tethering, too much commitment.

My eldest sister and her family lived in a two-bedroom a few floors up in the same building. My brother-in-law was completing his residency and worked thirty-six-hour shifts. My niece wasn't yet a year old and sometimes I brought her down to my apartment while my sister took a shower or ran to the store. I would sit on the floor and play with her and read to her. I loved that, too. Throughout my teens, I'd loathed the idea of a future and the work of planning for it. But I hadn't felt anything like the deep satisfaction I experienced soothing my niece to sleep.

I was pregnant within my first month of marriage, and my first son was born just after I turned nineteen. We bought a townhouse.

I had my second son when I was twenty-five, after losing a baby late term the year before. I wanted him so much that my chest was constricted throughout the pregnancy; I vibrated under my skin, clenched with longing.

When I held each of my children, I knew what to do. I liked to talk to them while I chopped vegetables, walk to the library and check out all the picture books on worms, meander with toddlers, make great messes with school-aged children, adopt a firm tone with teenagers. We made a big deal out of birthdays through invented ceremonies and traditions: breakfast in bed, small gifts wrapped individually. I felt so settled when we all sat down to a meal. In the car, windows down, music loud as we screamed the lyrics and laughed—I wanted for nothing.

When my first son was a toddler, I began a decade of haltingly taking classes at the local community college but withdrew whenever my family seemed to suffer from my absence. I was soft, prone to migraines, deeply distant from myself, committed to being a good parent. To being consistent, steady. I never worried about money aloud, or spoke ill of their father, never let them see me weep while stirring a pot on the stove. I paid attention to their interests, made sure they looked and smelled clean, ate balanced meals. I made up games and reward systems to help them do the things they didn't want to do. I was fun. I was bright. Parenthood demands we protect our children from the bald wound of our absolute terror, that we project a certain confidence about the future in order for them to go about the business of growing up.

I harbored a fantasy, though: to leave my family behind and start a new, simpler life, one in which I was not responsible for anyone else's experience of the world. I'd rent a studio apartment in a small Midwestern city and find work as a receptionist and wear the same five outfits every week. I imagined transferring the phone line to the machine at 5:00 p.m. on the dot, then going home to eat M&M's for dinner and read in bed in complete privacy, away from the needs of others, away from the pressure to be happy, to delight and entertain and soothe.

My marriage started on shaky ground and devolved quickly. He was angry; I was resentful. He tried to make me happy and was furious when I wasn't.

When we were nearing our tenth anniversary, I registered at a university in Vermont for a low-residency BFA in creative writing. In those eight days in Plainfield, I had meals in the cafeteria, access to a large library, and a responsibility to design a study plan for the coming semester. On large paper, I planned what I'd read, what I'd write—what I'd think about. For those days, my work was to live inside my own mind. To consider what I felt, what I thought. At home, in my daily life, silencing my thoughts and feelings was paramount to my survival, paramount to being a parent.

I bought a new copy of *My Wicked, Wicked Ways*, having lost the original. I opened it and the smoke of who I'd planned to be rose up.

I saved money, negotiated custody, and moved out with the bookshelf and a king-size bed my ex-husband didn't want. My new apartment was ten floors up in another high-rise. I woke before dawn most mornings, walked the few steps from the bedroom to the galley kitchen, where the coffee I'd set the night before brewed on a timer, hours before I had to wake the kids for school or be anywhere myself. I'd watch the sky lighten through the uncurtained, east-facing windows.

Sometimes, I'd walk the fifty yards down the green-carpeted hallway on Friday evening with a bag of groceries, and when the door clicked behind me, I'd turn the deadbolt, pull the chain, and remain inside, unseen, until Sunday. I'd tell everyone *I'm working on a very important project* and turn off the phone and internet.

I wrote two books in the silence of that apartment. I also ate a lot of edibles and gave myself orgasms and danced to Robyn and LCD Soundsystem and streamed a lot of television. When I'm alone, I can work or lie facedown and cry and no one knows the difference; no one is alarmed by my grief or astonished by my joy. Even as I type this, a decade into this arrangement, it seems miraculous. Wool over everyone's eyes.

One afternoon, I find myself in the same town as a person I like, our hands almost touching across the table. The yearning is sweet, harmless, theoretical. He compliments my sentences, my unflinching eye, my work in the world, my courage. Not a word about my hair or my smile or my shoulders sculpted by hot yoga.

He waits for a lull in the conversation and tells me he loves me. I look away. I love him, too. I love yearning for him, imagining him thinking of me. What flows between us is mutual admiration and a lack of demands. He waits a beat and says, "You write a lot about what would happen if someone *really* knew you. What are you so afraid of people knowing?"

1. I often forget to flush the toilet.
2. I respond to my enemies aloud while I roam my apartment.
3. I'm messy but frustrated by others' messes.
4. I smoke at least one cigarette a day.
5. I hate shaving my legs.
6. I'm annoyed if interrupted while looking out the window.

7. I eat microwaved nachos off a plate balanced on my chest at least once a week.
8. I resent communication if I'm occupied.
9. I'm not as much fun as anyone thinks I am.

My temper, I tell him.

But really, I mean: Under the blinking gaze of even one other person, I'm changed. I force a smile then seethe at the effort. It wasn't until a legal document ordered me to spend half my time without my children that I was able to finish school and build a career, one that depends on my willingness to experience my moods, to dive into the darkness and dwell in it.

"You will be the light of any house you go to," my mother used to say when I was happy.

"Why are you like this?" she would ask when I was unsmiling, or if I took a joke too personally.

To live with other people is to be responsible for protecting them from your moods. Or perhaps, to protect the delicate gift of your moods from them. Being fully myself requires that I stay in the deep and not bob to the surface when begged to emerge. In Apartment, in my apartment, I contend only with myself, with my own needs.

I don't know if I sleep better when I'm alone, but when I'm alone, I'm free to sleep poorly.

Tied, Tethered, Unfettered, Free
Melissa Faliveno

No tree, it turns out, is an island.
This body, I'm learning, isn't either.

Not long ago, in New York City, I was filling out a tax form for a teaching job in North Carolina. The position would be temporary. My partner, John—a high school teacher in Brooklyn—would stay in the apartment we'd shared for a decade.

I entered the basics—name, age, gender, Social Security number—these binary markers that, to the government and most people who live in this country, still define you as a person.

Then I got to "Marital Status." I stopped, considered my options. *Divorced. Widowed. Separated. Married. Single.* My pen hovered above the page. I've never been married, but I certainly don't think of myself as single.

I stared down at the words as if noticing them for the first time—rather than, of course, having been confronted with them my entire life.

When I was just a girl, I made a vow: I would never get married.

At its best, the whole enterprise seemed like a scam, one created and perpetuated by institutions like the church and the state, both of which I was already starting to distrust. At its worst, marriage seemed like a trap—one created specifically to ensnare women.

I swore I'd never bind myself to another person, least of all a man; I swore never to cede my independence, never to tie myself down.

Though I didn't believe in marriage, I did believe in love. I'd been in love—or at least what one thinks of as love when one is young, which is to say I'd yearned and longed and pined. I wrote love letters and folded them into little paper footballs, flicking them across classrooms with my heart in my throat. I watched rom-coms and cried (I still do). I read *Bop* and *Teen Beat*, hung posters of celebrity crushes on my wall. I read *Seventeen* and *YM* and circled outfits and makeup tips and hair-straightening techniques and make-out guides in hot pink highlighter.

I read *Sassy*, too—my former-hippie mother had gotten me a subscription, my earliest foray into feminism—and so I also learned not to subjugate my desires or principles for boys or men.

But I continued to love them anyway, getting my little heart pummeled again and again, several times quite cruelly. Like faith in God—which I still held on to then—I believed in love despite very little real-life evidence. In the marriages around me—working-class, Midwestern ones—I saw nothing of what I expected from the movies. Never affection, certainly never desire. Instead, I saw service and obligation. In fathers, I saw great wide gulfs of distance, physical and emotional. In mothers—who cooked every meal, who did the childcare and housework, even when they too had full-time jobs—I saw resentment, a distance of its own. I saw irritation, bickering, and anger. I saw silence, the worst of all.

I saw divorces, too, and wasn't sure which was worse. I watched friends shuffle off to their dads' places on Friday nights, back-packs stuffed with underwear and T-shirts. Sometimes I tagged along, spending weekends with one particular friend on her father's farm. Sometimes I snuck peeks at him in the living room, watching football and drinking beer, shirtless after a long day of work outside.

That doesn't look so bad, I thought.

My friend and I played in the barn, climbing a ladder to the hayloft. In our small hands we clutched a rope. It was frayed, some threads having begun to unspool from the root. But it was sturdy enough, we believed, to support us. We took a deep breath and held on tight, our hearts hammering in our chests. We took a running jump off the ledge.

For a moment, we were suspended. Then we fell, our stomachs in our throats, the breath knocked out of our lungs. And then a catch, and we were held, our bodies arcing through the air.

We swung. We flew. We were so free.

In my early twenties, I traveled for a time in the kink scene. I was never really into pain, but I did like submission—most frequently at the hands of men. This came as something of a shock: I was a budding bisexual in an androgynous body, leaning a little more masculine each day; a girl who'd grown up playing sports and lifting weights, who sought strength wherever she could find it. I was a woman who would soon start using the words *gender-nonconforming* and *genderqueer*, who would soon fall in love with a woman, who fancied herself far more top than bottom, who was starting to suspect that to move through the world a little more like a man could be a form of power, too.

But at the time, I was also suffering from severe anxiety, my days pulsing to the unpredictable beat of panic. That I'd recently begun to lose the religion I'd grown up with was probably no coincidence. I was aware, for the first time in my life, of what it meant to be alone, to be vulnerable, to fall through the world without the safety net of faith.

When a lover first bound my wrists to a bedpost with two silk ties, I was calm. When I first tried Shibari—Japanese rope bondage originating from a form of captive torture—the practitioner, or "Rigger," tied me to a chair in a nightclub. He wound and looped and pulled, the ropes cutting into my bare shoulders and chest. My breath got tight. For a second or two I panicked. But then the tension gave way, dissolving into surrender.

I found something like solace in restriction, release in being bound. I felt myself let go. My brain, always racing, went quiet. I heard only the hum of the club, the drum of my heart.

When I met John, I fell in love fast. He was funny, handsome, and smart, an artist and musician who would eventually become a bandmate. I'd moved from Wisconsin to New York a year earlier but was only recently untethered from a long relationship with a terrible end. I was heartbroken and traumatized, pretty sure I was done with men (or at least straight, cisgender men) forever.

The first weekend we spent together, John asked me to be his girlfriend. It was sudden, and sweet, and I found it wildly old-fashioned. We hadn't even slept together. I knew I liked him, but I was hesitant.

I sat on a cheap IKEA bed in an apartment I shared with two roommates in Yonkers. He'd taken the train up from the city to see me, something he would do daily for the better part of a year until we moved in together in Brooklyn.

He was nervous, and hopeful, and so was I.

"Maybe let's wait a little while and see," I said.

"You gotta lock that down," people say, as if to partner is not to join someone in life but to hold them captive. I hear language like this—as well as "tie the knot" and "get hitched"—and roll my eyes. What an idea, to tie someone up in order to make them yours.

In 2015, John and I bought a blanket from a Montauk gift shop and laid it on the beach. It was late October, and dusk, and we watched dark waves crash onto shore. We built a fire and drank champagne, toasting five years together and many more to come.

We stayed in an old hotel, nearly empty in the off-season. It was done up for Halloween, cotton cobwebs dotted with little plastic spiders strung from stairs to front desk. John bought me a professional massage, the first I'd ever had, and afterward my body was buzzing. I floated back to our room and found him there: lights off, candle lit, a picture out of a movie.

"I have something for you," he said, and pulled out a black velvet box.

"Wait!" I said. "I have something for you!"

I scrambled to my bag and pulled out a little black box of my own.

We laughed. We opened our boxes at the same time, presenting one another the rings. We slid them on each other's fingers. The one he'd picked for me was gold; the one I'd picked for him was silver. It was etched with a rope—not knotted, but loose at both ends. A symbol, I told him, of our life together—not in a traditional sense, maybe, but something better. We would not be tied to each other, but rather we would hold on to both ends, a conscious act of connection.

I never wanted to be anyone's wife. To be a *wife*, I'd learned—in church, and at so many Midwestern weddings—was to be owned. Women were put on Earth to serve their husbands, then serve as a vessel; it was their duty to procreate, then go on serving. Marriage was a command of God, a conduit for kids, a life sentence for any woman who wanted something more. Women weren't lovers, and they certainly weren't partners. They were wives and mothers. This was their purpose.

I refused to buy in. Part of this refusal has always been bound to my identity—as a feminist, as a queer person in a queer body—and part is bound to fear: that to get married, especially to a man, would mean erasing part of myself. That I would be turning in my queer card, falling in line. That even as I struggle against the confines of gender, I would still be held in its grip. That, in the end, I would just be another woman married to a man.

Growing up, I sometimes watched my parents get dressed for work. My mother put on bright-colored blouses and skirts, matching pumps in teal and red and blue, blazers with massive shoulder pads. She was beautiful, confident, and strong, but always unquestionably feminine—the look of a Marshall's store manager who spent hours unloading trucks in Wisconsin winters in heels, her hair-sprayed curls frozen in place. Crouched in her closet, I organized her leather rainbow of shoes.

In those days, my father was a salesman. He was successful and charming, often on the road to Dayton and Des Moines, always in a suit. Sitting on my parents' bed, I watched him fasten his necktie in front of a full-length mirror. This was the late eighties and early nineties, so of course the ties were hideous: wide, patterned things sprayed with bright geometric shapes, like the ones on my Trapper Keeper.

Maybe he tried to teach me how to tie them, but I only remember watching. He stood close to the mirror, crisp white shirt against olive skin, and tied the knot—chin up, hair dark, handsome. I remember thinking how strange a tie was: this soft, pretty thing that men tightened up to the throat. Such a curious custom, for a man to constrict himself this way.

I was in my early twenties when I first put on a tie. It was skinny and silk and black, and my lover at the time, a man who wore one himself every day, taught me how to tie it.

"Double Windsor for spread collars," he said, standing behind me in the bathroom mirror. "Single Windsor for straight."

I nodded, brow crunched, pulling the wide end to my belt, skinny end to my belly button. I popped the fold of silk in my mouth and looped it through, then pulled it tight. I put on a blazer over my shirt—point collar and single-Windsor for the neck of a girl, a word I still used to describe myself then.

It would be a few more years before I got rid of all my dresses and skirts and heels. But that day, standing in front of the mirror, I liked what I saw: white shirt against olive skin, I tightened the knot—chin up, hair dark, handsome.

For a long time, I told John that if we ever did get married, it wouldn't be until gay people could. Most of my closest friends are queer, and if I'd been with a woman, I wouldn't have been able to get married anyway. I firmly believed in this principle, and still do. But to a certain extent, I also hid behind it. As long as the laws didn't change, I wouldn't have to confront the future of my own partnership.

But in the summer of 2015, when the Supreme Court struck down the marriage ban in all fifty states, I went to Stonewall and celebrated in the streets with my friends. And then I bought the ring.

When I think back to this decision, I don't remember it being a question. I only remember watching so many friends who'd been in relationships for years or even decades finally get engaged, or head directly to the courthouse. I remember relief, and hope, and joy. Maybe I got caught up in all of it; maybe we all did.

But I also began to understand, for the first time, that to enter into an inherently heteronormative institution as a queer person didn't have to mean assimilating; it could be in itself a radical act: I would buy the ring, and I would be the one to propose. I would resist the traditional expectations placed upon me as a woman, forgo the words *engagement* and *fiancé*, *husband* and *wife*. If I were going to do this, I would queer it as best I could.

Lia Purpura writes, "All the fierce tethers to all the fierce moments—they matter, to the pinpoint I've become."

I used to think I was meant to be alone. That if I found myself tethered, I would be the one to leave. I would live in the woods, just me and my books and the trees, as it was always destined to be. I built this narrative for myself, told this story so often I believed it.

But this story is not just about independence. Part of it is rooted in self-preservation. Part of it is fear. The truth is that I'm afraid of being alone. Another truth is that I've never been alone for long. And while I certainly thrive in solitude, I'm also a creature of partnership. I want the limbs of my beloved next to me—entangled with mine, always within reach.

As time passed with John, I learned for the first time how to trust another person. To not assume I would be hurt or left. We made music and art, adopted pets, split chores down the middle, encouraged and supported each other. He read my writing and I wrote harmonies for his songs. When we sang together, our voices were a perfect fit. We laughed every day. We started talking about how our wedding might look. But I would often cut those conversations short, anxious about the planning and still conflicted about what I felt and what I believed—about those old messages from church, about the state, about all the patriarchal, misogynistic, heteronormative institutions that were never built for me.

It's been several years since that weekend in Montauk, and we're still not married. We didn't tell our parents about the rings, and we didn't tell many of our friends. I'm still not sure why.

But John wears his ring every day, on his left pinky. Once in a while I wear mine. I wanted to save it until after the wedding, but sometimes I put it on anyway—especially when I'm without him, when I want to feel closer to him and closer to home. I wear it on my right ring finger—a small, silent resistance to the norm, a nod to queer elders, devoid of the implications carried by a gold band on the left hand of a woman.

The rope etching on John's ring was supposed to be permanent. Or at least I assumed it was. But now it's nearly gone—worn down by years and the daily touch of skin, faded to almost nothing. Unless you look close enough, you might never know it was there. We asked a jeweler if it could be polished back into shape, if there was some kind of secret buffing technique that could miraculously make the rope resurface. They told us the fading is normal, that there's nothing they could do.

I felt cheated, lied to, betrayed. By the jeweler, by my own stupid certainty. The ring was a promise, and it was one I believed.

These days, it's hard not to think of permanence and impermanence. About liminal and tenuous states. These days, life seems a little more fragile. Or maybe we're just feeling its edges more fully. We spend so much of our lives trying to make things stay, convincing ourselves they will. We believe that we can keep what's ours if we just work hard enough; if we just lock down our doors, board up our windows, and stay inside with our own. That if we just hold on tightly enough to our families and homes and lives, we'll survive.

Belief is a funny thing, especially in times of great uncertainty. But of course, it's hopeful, too. Even though I'm agnostic now, there are some things from growing up in church that stay with me. I know, for instance, that faith is a way to hold on to hope and give meaning to our lives—which is really all any of us are trying to do. And maybe, like faith, there are some things—despite what intellectual understanding tells us—we just can't help but believe in.

John and I are in a state of limbo. As I write this, we're apart: I'm in the woods of North Carolina, and he's in New York. We're trying to figure it out. In one version of the future, we're together. In another, we're not.

He wants kids; I'm not sure if I do. A year ago, I was sure I didn't, and I was sure he'd choose me anyway, that he'd choose me over anything. I was sure about what I wanted; I was sure about our future. Now I'm not sure of anything.

I sit alone at my desk and take my ring out of its box. I slide it onto my right hand. I spin it around. It needs a good cleaning—a few fast strokes of a scrub pad to make it good as new.

I take the ring off, put it back in its box. I take it out again, put it back on. I can't bear the weight of it. I can't bear the emptiness without it.

I find myself wishing I hadn't dragged my feet when we talked about our wedding. I wish I hadn't gotten so stressed every time we discussed the guest list. I wish I had just said, "Yes. Let's do this." Not because I think it would make this decision easier. Not because I believe anyone can be locked down. But maybe because I want, if only for a while, to believe in forever. Maybe because I know that when the logistics of release are easier, we're bound to let go.

I've been thinking about roots and limbs. About the idea of *putting down roots*. Of ending a life of limbo, taking a stab at something permanent. It's a societal trick, sure. But there's a reason most people buy in. We plant our little lives in the ground, our roots reaching deeper into the earth—seeking purchase, solidity, having faith it won't all come down in a windstorm, that we'll keep on standing.

The words *limb* and *limbo* share the same root. Limbo, of

course, is a place of transition. Of confinement or restraint. Uncertainty or oblivion. An existential waiting room. It's a place of fear, but also hope: that one might ascend rather than fall.

And *limb*: an arm, a leg, a wing, a branch—something malleable and movable. A thing meant to bend and bow, but that so often does not break. In the western United States, there's a tree called the limber pine—*Pinus flexilis*—named for its especially pliant branches. Found mostly in the mountains, it's meant to withstand harsh conditions. It's made, of course, to bend.

Women, too, are conditioned to bend. To put the needs of others—men, children, anyone but themselves—before their own, to carry the weight and not break. One of my first lessons of feminism was to resist this. To be a strong, independent, queer woman is to defy the things we're taught women should be, to dismantle the expectations pressed down upon us. To do this work, we fight for our desires. We put them first, even when we're called selfish. Even when we believe ourselves selfish, too. This is how I've been able to pursue my career, become a writer, live a life I never thought possible: a dogged focus on putting those desires first. I veered from the path of tradition—one that might have been more comfortable, more certain—to carve one of my own.

And now I find myself bending. The way ahead that always looked clear now seems impassable, indistinct. I see the desires of the person I love and want him to be happy. I'm imagining new forms happiness might take. I'm imagining, for the first time, what it might look like to be a mother. Sometimes I hate what I see, and sometimes I don't. But I can't figure out what I want. I can't hide from the fact that I'm peering down a path I've always resisted because it's where a man wants to go. Whether this makes me a bad feminist or a better partner, I'm not sure.

I've always been bad at making decisions. I hem and haw, fret and agonize, much to the chagrin of anyone who has ever loved me. So often, when I try to discover the truth of what I feel—to follow my heart, to trust my gut—I find I feel nothing at all. This ambivalence has old, deep roots. To make a choice, I learned, to make a commitment, is to have faith. And to have faith means letting go, ceding control, relying on and believing in something, or someone, other than yourself. Even, or perhaps especially, when you know that almost everyone—not least those you trust—will eventually let you down.

People keep telling me to have faith. To take a leap of faith. To keep the faith. To trust in the process—of writing, of living, of love—and jump. But I find myself stuck to the earth. And even planted here, in this ground I sowed myself, these roots don't feel firm. Rather than feeling solid, they only feel unsure—buried shallow, reaching up through the soil.

Sometimes, I imagine our wedding. It would be a small affair, maybe in the woods of Wisconsin or Upstate New York, with a few of our closest family and friends. It would be a queer affair, too. I would wear a suit and stand beside my love in his. I don't wear ties much anymore these days; I've come to hate the tightness on my neck and prefer my collared shirts unbuttoned—throat bare, vulnerable, open. And maybe what I mean by that open collar, by that quick glimpse of clavicle and spray of freckles on my chest, is that I feel more feminine. Or maybe what I mean is that I just feel a little more like me.

Whoever married us—a friend, probably, a writer or musician—wouldn't talk of God or the state or *man and wife*. They wouldn't talk of duty or possession or the vessel of my body. They would talk of partnership, commitment, community, and love. Of choosing a path and following it together, whatever might come. We wouldn't recite Bible passages or sing hymns, but if we spoke of forever, it might sound a lot like a prayer.

A year or so ago, at John's parents' house in Ohio, we sat on the floor by the fire.

"I hope you two get married," his mother said to me.

I know it came from a place of love. John's family is more traditional than mine, and certainly more religious; I know marriage, to them, would make me more firmly a part of the family. But I couldn't help but hear, "I hope you make it *real*." As if without a ring on the correct finger—without a certificate or kids or the labels *husband* and *wife*—a partnership, a love, a life of ten years together is nothing. It's impermanent and fleeting, not etched in silver or stone. It might as well not exist.

But what I said was, "I hope so, too."

It's late November, and the woods around me—so recently full and green and alive—are now stripped bare. At night, where there was once the song of crickets, the rush of wind in leaves, there is only the tapping of branches against my windows. Whole limbs have snapped off in late fall storms. And I see myself among these trees: the solitary oak, the barren maple.

I've been thinking about loneliness, and aloneness. I've been alone like this before, but I've never been more lonely. My friends and family scattered around the country, my love five hundred miles north. In the past, when I spent time alone in the woods, I always had my home, and my life, to return to. In those woods of my past, I was happy. But now, morning comes slow and night falls fast. I don't find calm, only the closeness of the forest. In an empty bed I reach for a phantom limb and touch only the dark arms of night. I imagine its branches pulling me into the loam, burying me in the dirt. Where they might hold me, keep me, never let me go.

Yesterday I took a walk. I followed a path that I'd taken a few weeks before, when John had come to visit. We'd stopped in a clearing as the sun began to fall; the path was buried in a soft brown carpet of leaves and pine needles, and we decided to turn back. This time I pressed on, following the trail to its end, where I discovered a stream. I looked up and saw vines wrapped around tall pines, calcified and fused to the trunks. There were trees and branches scattered all around, the product of a recent storm. On a young oak, still standing, a large branch had snapped off. I touched the soft and open wood. Soon, in that place, there would be a knot.

Not long ago I learned that trees do not function in isolation. A tree may appear to stand alone, but she is, in fact, part of an intricate network. Deep in the soil, her roots fasten to those of her neighbors. They talk to one another, protect one another, function as a team. Far beyond what we can see, there's a complex system, a commune that keeps the forest alive.

No tree, it turns out, is an island. This body, I'm learning, isn't either.

I don't know how to tie many knots, but I've learned a few. A bow-line, a clove hitch, a reef knot. How to secure a boat to a dock, how to tie a Canaan fir to the roof of a truck. There are the kind of knots that bind, and there are the kind that bend. As he tied me up, the Shibari Rigger—following tradition, a man, like most people who have taught me how to tie things—showed me the knots one can use on a body: those that can be slipped off, and those that cannot. He taught me how to hold another person, and how to set them free.

When I encountered the Marital Status section on that tax form, it carried a new kind of weight. In the past, I knew *single* was just an institutional term. In the eyes of the government, sure, I was on my own. But I knew my knot was tied. Now, I wonder what it might look like for the rope to be severed, for *single* to mean *alone*. Would it feel like falling—might it feel free? Would I choose, again, to tie myself to another person, or might I remain forever unbound?

In August 2015, two months after the Supreme Court ruling and two months before our trip to Montauk, John and I drove across the country. We traveled from New York to New Mexico, camping in North Carolina, Tennessee, Oklahoma, and Texas. We were headed to the wedding of our good friend Jessica, the woman who had introduced us. John would be a bridesman, and I would officiate the ceremony.

At first, when Jessica asked me to officiate, I was conflicted. I didn't even know if I believed in marriage; was it morally conscionable to wed my friends? But I was honored, and excited, and of course I said yes. I spent two minutes on the internet, filling out a form on the Universal Life Church website. I sent $29.99 via PayPal, and a few weeks later received a certificate, an ID card, and a bumper sticker in the mail. I was officially an ordained minister. Most of my family found this very funny.

All summer, I wrote and rewrote and revised the ceremony. I interviewed the couple, together and alone, asking them each what they wanted, what they hoped for, what they feared. What marriage meant to them. How they knew. I was asking for them, but I think now that I was also asking for me.

On the road, I practiced my speech. I read it aloud to John.

"Is it good?" I asked.

"It's perfect," he said.

I looked at him as he drove, and maybe it was all the romance of what I was writing, or the promise of our friend finding love— knowing that so many of my friends could now do this, too—but for a moment, fast as the summer light flashing in through the trees, I knew what I wanted.

And at the wedding, high in the Sandia Mountains, somewhere between Albuquerque and Santa Fe, I married my friends. I wore a suit, but I didn't wear a tie. I didn't speak of God or the state. I didn't speak of service or duty. I spoke, instead, of partnership and commitment and love. I spoke of the community gathered there: that this, too, was our vow—that this bind was ours to keep and protect. I spoke of two people, not owned by the other, not bound or tied or tethered but maybe, somehow, more free.

Some days I still wear the ring John gave me, and some days I don't. When I do, I still wear it on my right ring finger. Some days, though, when I'm alone, I slide it onto my left. My right hand is stronger, dominant; on an androgynous body, I think of it as my more masculine side. My left hand is smaller, and the ring doesn't fit as well there. It's a little loose, and I'm afraid it might fall off, that I might look one day to find it gone. But I like the way it feels there. I like the weight of it. Maybe I even like feeling bound to another person, feeling claimed. Or maybe I just want to believe that something will remain.

I don't know if John and I will get married. I don't know if we'll last forever, or if we'll even make it to next year. I hope we do. That day in the mountains, I wasn't sure how I felt about marriage. In many ways I'm still not. But I do know that as I stood in front of my friends and said those words aloud, I believed them.

There are a few other things I know: That I want to make things for the world that might do some good. That I want to be near the people I love. That I want a partner to walk beside me through the woods or a city street, as long as life allows. I don't know if I'll be a mother. Maybe, if my thoughts on marriage have changed, my thoughts on kids might, too. Maybe they won't. I don't know, but I'm trying to be open to the possibility. I'm trying to embrace the unknown. I'm trying to trust the process, and I'm trying to have faith. I'm trying to hold on to this rope, and I'm trying to let go.

Acknowledgments

Eliza would like to thank Barb, Miki, and Gwynn, a trio of single mothers, for teaching her almost everything she knows about life; her nieces, Kerrigan and Annie, for bringing her immeasurable joy; Teddy, for keeping Haley fed and happy; Julie, Alaina, and Amanda, for their Big Friendship (to borrow from Aminatou Sow and Ann Friedman); her English 1100 students for showing her how much there is to say about singlehood; Sari Botton and Catapult for the crash course in anthologies; Dawn and Rick for their love; and Sheldon (and the cats) for being home.

Haley would like to thank Rick, Laurie, Mikey, and Enzo, the best home base she could ever ask for; Hillary, Katie, Emi, Mona, and Emmy, for being her writing safe space; Molly and Jaimie, for the same and so much more; Sheldon, for making Eliza laugh and for creating a book trailer that is both incredible and should never see the light of day; Marita for the food and Michael for the wine; Emma, Sarah, and Mary for litmus testing covers and emails alike; and Theo, for everything, always.

Together, we would also like to thank our incredible agent Allison Hunter as well as Natalie Edwards for being our earliest and strongest supporters, and the formidable Emily Griffin for leading the charge. Thanks, too, to everyone else at Harper: Micaela Carr, Megan Looney, Suzette Lam, Amy Baker, and Doug Jones. Thanks a million times over to Kristina Moore, Jessica Calagione, and Kazumi Fish. To Heather Brown at Mind the Bird Media, thank you for connecting so immediately and completely with this project. We would've been lost without your help. And a heartfelt *efcharistó* to the Writing Workshops in Greece for bringing us together.

Last but not least, endless gratitude to our contributors, whose words (literally and emotionally) charted the course of this journey.

About the Editors

Eliza Smith's work has appeared in *The Cut*, *The Offing*, *Indiana Review*, and elsewhere and has been awarded an Ohio Arts Council Individual Excellence Award. She earned her MA in magazine writing from the Missouri School of Journalism and MFA in creative nonfiction from Ohio State. She currently works as the special projects editor at Literary Hub.

Haley Swanson is a writer and editor based in New York. Her essays have appeared in *The Rumpus*, *Glamour*, *Electric Literature*, *Creative Nonfiction*, *Brevity*, and elsewhere. She's an MFA candidate at Sarah Lawrence College.

About the Contributors

Samantha Allen is the author of *Patricia Wants to Cuddle* (Zando, 2022) and the Lambda Literary Award finalist *Real Queer America: LGBT Stories from Red States*. She is a GLAAD Award–winning journalist whose writing has been published by *The New York Times*, *Rolling Stone*, CNN, and more. She lives with her wife and hairless cats in Seattle.

Kristen Arnett is the author of *With Teeth: A Novel* (Riverhead Books, 2021) and *The New York Times* bestselling debut novel *Mostly Dead Things* (Tin House, 2019), which was a finalist for the Lambda Literary Award in fiction. She is a queer fiction and essay writer. She was awarded *Ninth Letter*'s Literary Award in Fiction, has been a columnist for *Literary Hub*, and is a current columnist for *Catapult*. She was a spring 2020 Shearing Fellow at Black Mountain Institute. Her work has appeared in *The New York Times*, *The Cut, O, the Oprah Magazine, Guernica, BuzzFeed, McSweeney's, PBS Newshour, The Guardian, Salon,* and elsewhere. Her next book (an untitled collection of short stories) will be published by Riverhead Books (Penguin Random House). She has a master's in library and information science from Florida State University and currently lives in Miami, Florida.

Laura Bogart is the author of the novel *Don't You Know I Love You* (Dzanc Books, 2020). Her work has appeared in *The Atlantic*, *Salon*, *DAME*, *Vulture*, *BuzzFeed*, and *The Week*.

Keah Brown is an actress, journalist, author, and screenwriter. She is the creator of #DisabledAndCute. Her work has appeared in *Teen Vogue*, *Elle*, *Harper's Bazaar*, *Marie Claire UK*, and *The New York Times*, among other publications. Her debut essay collection, *The Pretty One*, is out now. Her debut picture book, *Sam's Super Seats*, will be out in 2022 via Kokila, an imprint of Penguin Random House. Find out more at keahbrown.com.

Jennifer Chowdhury is a journalist and writer dedicated to stories on migration and immigration with a special focus on women of color around the world whose voices are stifled by patriarchy, systematic racism, and socioeconomic burdens. She spent two years reporting on the Rohingya refugee crisis in Bangladesh. Her work has been featured in *The Washington Post*, NPR, *The Guardian*, *The New York Times*, *Elle*, and more.

Tiana Clark is the author of the poetry collection *I Can't Talk About the Trees Without the Blood* (University of Pittsburgh Press, 2018), winner of the 2017 Agnes Lynch Starrett Prize, and *Equilibrium* (Bull City Press, 2016), selected by Afaa Michael Weaver for the 2016 Frost Place Chapbook Competition. Clark is a winner of the 2020 Kate Tufts Discovery Award (Claremont Graduate University), a 2019 National Endowment for the Arts Literature Fellow, a recipient of a 2019 Pushcart Prize, a winner of the 2017 Furious Flower's Gwendolyn Brooks Centennial Poetry Prize, and the 2015 Rattle Poetry Prize. She was the 2017–2018 Jay C. and Ruth Halls Poetry Fellow at the Wisconsin Institute of Creative Writing. Her writing has appeared in or is forthcoming from *The New Yorker*, *The Atlantic*, *Poetry Magazine*, *The Washington Post*, *Tin House Online*, *Kenyon Review*, *BuzzFeed News*, *American Poetry Review*, *Oxford American*, and elsewhere. She is the Grace Hazard Conkling Writer-in-Residence at Smith College.

Kate Crawford was fifteen when Helen Gurley Brown's *Sex and the Single Girl* came out. By the time she read it in college, she already knew she would have sex as a single. (She was, however, surprised at her fiftieth reunion with how many women admitted they'd married simply because they were having sex with the man.) Kate started writing in 2000. Her work has appeared in *The Washington Post*, *The Boston Globe*, *San Francisco Chronicle*, and *Best Travel Writing 2012*. She's been honored with awards from the Tucson Festival of Books, Taos Writers, Solas, Wanderlust and Lipstick, and Book Passage's Travel Writers. She owned, wrote for, and photographed the now-defunct website *Ciao! Travel with Attitude*, which attained a hundred thousand hits a month. Kate lives in senior cohousing where everything, except the seniors, is sustainable.

Evette Dionne is a journalist, pop-culture critic, and magazine editor. She's the National Book Award–nominated and Coretta Scott King Honor author of *Lifting as We Climb: Black Women's Battle for the Ballot Box*, and she currently works on Netflix's editorial team. Evette writes extensively about pop culture through the lenses of race, gender, and size for a number of print and digital publications, including NBC News, *Cosmopolitan*, *Glamour*, *Time*, *The New York Times*, *Guardian*, *SELF*, and *Harper's Bazaar*. You can find her across the web at @freeblackgirl.

Rosemary Donahue is a writer, editor, and a third thing that is constantly changing. They live in Brooklyn, New York, with their dog, Milo.

Melissa Faliveno is the author of the essay collection *TOMBOY-LAND*, which was named a Best Book of 2020 by NPR, the New York Public Library, *O, the Oprah Magazine*, and *Electric Literature*, and received a 2021 award for outstanding literary achievement from the Wisconsin Library Association. Her essays and interviews have appeared in *Esquire*, *Paris Review*, *Bitch*, *Ms.*, *Lit Hub*, *Brooklyn Rail*, and *Prairie Schooner*, among others, and received a notable selection in *Best American Essays*. The former senior editor of *Poets & Writers Magazine*, she was the 2020–21 Kenan Visiting Writer at the University of North Carolina in Chapel Hill and is currently a visiting assistant professor of English at Kenyon College. You can find her online at melissafaliveno.com.

Melissa Febos is the author of the memoir *Whip Smart* and three essay collections: *Abandon Me*, a LAMBDA Literary Award and Publishing Triangle Award finalist; *Girlhood*, a national best-seller; and *Body Work: The Radical Power of Personal Narrative*. Febos is the inaugural winner of the Jeanne Córdova Nonfiction Award from LAMBDA Literary and the recipient of fellowships from the National Endowment for the Arts, MacDowell, Bread Loaf, Lower Manhattan Cultural Council, the BAU Institute, Vermont Studio Center, the Barbara Deming Foundation, and others; her essays have appeared in *The Paris Review*, *The Believer*, *McSweeney's Quarterly*, *Granta*, *Sewanee Review*, *Tin House*, *The Sun*, and *The New York Times*. She is an associate professor at the University of Iowa, where she teaches in the Nonfiction Writing Program.

Vanessa Friedman (she/her) is a queer dyke writer living in Portland, Oregon. She's the community editor at *Autostraddle* and a teaching artist with Literary Arts and 826NYC. She received her MFA in creative nonfiction from Sarah Lawrence College, and she is a Tin House Summer Workshop alum and a Hedgebrook Spring Retreat alum. Vanessa writes about friendship, home, loneliness, grief, sex, and the body; her work has been published in *Autostraddle*, *Nylon*, *Catapult*, *Alma*, *Shape*, and elsewhere. Vanessa is currently at work on her first novel. You can find her online at vanessapamela.com.

Brooke Hauser is a longtime journalist. She is the former editor in chief of the *Daily Hampshire Gazette* newspaper in Northampton, Massachusetts. She is also the author of two books: *Enter Helen: The Invention of Helen Gurley Brown and the Rise of the Modern Single Woman*, winner of the National Arts and Entertainment Journalism Award for Best Nonfiction Book, and *The New Kids: Big Dreams and Brave Journeys at a High School for Immigrant Teens*, a winner of the American Library Association's Alex Award. Hauser has written for *Allure*, *Marie Claire*, *The Boston Globe*, *The New York Times*, and *The New Yorker* online, among many other publications. For several years, she covered the film industry as a writer and editor at *Premiere*. Originally from Miami, Florida, Hauser lives with her family in western Massachusetts, where she has taught nonfiction writing at Smith College.

Minda Honey is a writer from Louisville, Kentucky. She has let men in every time zone break her heart. Related: *An Anthology of Assholes*, her essay collection about dating as a woman of color, is forthcoming from Little A in summer 2023. Her writing has appeared in *Longreads*, *The Guardian*, *The Undefeated*, *Salon*, the *Oxford American*, and elsewhere.

Briallen Hopper is the author of *Hard to Love: Essays and Confessions*, a Kirkus Best Book of 2019. She teaches creative writing at Queens College, CUNY, and lives in Elmhurst, Queens, with a thousand books and a hundred dresses.

Giaae Kwon's writing has appeared in *Catapult*, *The Rumpus*, *Buzz-Feed Reader*, *Electric Literature*, and *Taste*. She writes the newsletter *I Love You, Egg*, and lives in Brooklyn.

Tawny Lara is a New York City–based writer whose work examines the intersection of sobriety and sexuality. Her words are published in *Playboy*, *Men's Health*, and *HuffPost*, and she cohosts the *Recovery Rocks* podcast. Fun fact: she has a spicy taco dish named after her ("La Chica Diabla") in her hometown of Waco, Texas.

Shayla Lawson is that bitch. You can find more words at her regular column for *Bustle* magazine or in her 2020 essay collection *This Is Major: Notes on Diana Ross, Dark Girls, and Being Dope* (Harper Perennial, 2020).

Natalie Lima is a Cuban-Puerto Rican writer from Las Vegas, Nevada, and Hialeah, Florida. She is a first-generation college graduate of Northwestern University and a graduate of the MFA program in creative nonfiction writing at the University of Arizona. Her essays and fiction have been published or are forthcoming in *Longreads*, *Guernica*, *Catapult*, *Brevity*, *The Offing*, *Body Language* (Catapult, 2022), and elsewhere. She has received fellowships from PEN America Emerging Voices, Bread Loaf, Tin House, the VONA/Voices Workshop, the Virginia G. Piper Center for Creative Writing, and a residency from Hedgebrook. Natalie is currently working on a memoir in essays. You can find her on Instagram and Twitter @natalielima09.

Morgan Parker is a poet, essayist, and novelist. She is the author of the California Book Award–nominated young adult novel *Who Put This Song On?* and the poetry collections *Other People's Comfort Keeps Me Up at Night*, *There Are More Beautiful Things Than Beyoncé*, and *Magical Negro*, which won the 2019 National Book Critics Circle Award and California Book Award. Her debut book of nonfiction is forthcoming from One World. Parker's work has appeared in such publications as *The Paris Review*, *The New York Times*, *The New York Review of Books*, *Time*, *Best American Poetry*, and *Playbill*. She is the recipient of a National Endowment for the Arts Literature Fellowship, winner of a Pushcart Prize, a Cave Canem graduate fellow, and cofounder of the Other Black Girl Collective with Angel Nafis. Morgan lives in Los Angeles.

Nichole Perkins is a writer and podcast host from Nashville, Tennessee. She hosts *This Is Good for You*, a podcast about finding pleasure in life, and previously was a cohost of *Thirst Aid Kit*, a podcast about pop culture and desire. Nichole is the author of *Lilith, But Dark*, a poetry collection, and *Sometimes I Trip on How Happy We Could Be*, a memoir.

Josie Pickens is a professor, writer, cultural critic, storyteller, and radio host whose many works focus on race and gender, and the varying intersections of the two. Her ultimate goal is to serve as witness and to give voice to marginalized communities that often go unseen and unheard, through her gifts of interviewing, writing, documenting, and storytelling. Pickens has regularly provided timely social commentary for *Ebony*, *Essence*, and *Bitch* magazines, and she has been cited on *The New York Times* and *The Guardian* news sites. Pickens's current passion project is called *The Love No Limit Show* (a radio show that is also streamed as a podcast), which serves as a community forum and storytelling project that hopes to explore love in expansive, radical, restorative, and authentic ways. The questions the show works to answer (in varying ways) are: How do BIPOC people practice healthily loving ourselves, our romantic and platonic partners, our families, and our communities in the face of oppression, racism, sexism, homophobia, xenophobia, and more; and how do BIPOC people love and nurture our gifts and passions while facing the aforementioned kinds of complications? Find out more about Josie by visiting her website: www.josiepickens.me.

Xoài PhĐm is a Vietnamese trans woman descended from a long legacy of warriors, healers, and shamans. Her life's work is in dreaming new futures where we are all limitless. She makes those dreams a reality as a poet, essayist, editor, and screenwriter. She is currently the deputy director of communications at Transgender Law Center and trans subject editor of *Autostraddle*, while also writing for publications like *Elle*, *Esquire*, and *Teen Vogue*.

Seema Reza is a writer and performer and the author of *When the World Breaks Open* (Red Hen Press, 2016) and *A Constellation of*

Half-Lives (Write Bloody Publishing, 2019). Based outside of Washington, D.C., she is the CEO of Community Building Art Works, an organization that encourages the use of the arts as a tool for narration, self-care, and socialization among a military population struggling with emotional and physical injuries. In 2015 she was awarded the Colonel John Gioia Patriot Award by USO of Metropolitan Washington-Baltimore for her work with servicemembers. In 2018, the HBO documentary *We Are Not Done Yet* featured the work of Community Building Art Works. She has taught poetry in classrooms, jails, hospitals, and universities. An alumnus of Goddard College and VONA, her writing has appeared online and in print in *McSweeney's*, *The Washington Post*, *The LA Review*, *The Feminist Wire*, *HerKind*, *The Offing*, and *Entropy*, among others, and she has authored case studies that have appeared in *Post-Traumatic Stress Disorder and Related Diseases in Combat Veterans*. She has performed at universities, festivals, correctional facilities, and theaters across the country.